BOHEMIA IN LONDON

BOHEMIA IN LONDON

BY

ARTHUR RANSOME

ILLUSTRATIONS BY FRED TAYLOR

With an Introduction by
RUPERT HART-DAVIS

Oxford New York
OXFORD UNIVERSITY PRESS
1984

Oxford University Press, Walton Street, Oxford OX2 6DP

London Glasgow New York Toronto
Delhi Bombay Calcutta Madras Karachi
Kuala Lumpur Singapore Hong Kong Tokyo
Nairobi Dar es Salaam Cape Town
Melbourne Auckland

and associated companies in
Beirut Berlin Ibadan Mexico City Nicosia

First published by Chapman & Hall Limited 1907
First issued as an Oxford University Press paperback 1984

British Library Cataloguing in Publication Data

Ransome, Arthur
Bohemia in London.
1. London (England)—History—1800–1950
I. Title
942.1082′092′4 DA684
ISBN 0–19–281412–5

Printed in Great Britain by
Richard Clay (The Chaucer Press) Ltd.
Bungay, Suffolk

TO

M. P. SHIEL

NOTE

This book would never have been begun if it had not been for the friendly suggestion of Miss Ocean Lee. It would never have been finished but for the strenuous scolding and encouragement of Mr. Hughes Massie. It would be worse than it is if my friends, especially Mr. Edward Thomas, had been less generous of their advice.

Carlyle Studios. *July 1907*

CONTENTS

CONTENTS

CONCLUSION

INTRODUCTION

ARTHUR RANSOME was a very young twenty-two when he wrote this book. He had come down from his home in the North to seek his literary fortune in London. An eight-shillings-a-week job as office-boy to the rising publisher Grant Richards (whose fine literary taste eventually proved no match for his financial ineptitude) had introduced Ransome to the exciting world of books and their authors. He had published two very slim and feeble volumes of essays (which he spent the rest of his life trying to forget and destroy) and four tiny books for children, but *Bohemia in London* was 'a stout grey volume, looking like a real book, of which I was extremely proud'; moreover it was published by Dickens's old publishers Chapman & Hall, and its appearance in September 1907, only a few weeks after he had finished writing it (those were the days!), was the cause of great rejoicing.

After staying with friends and relations he had found an empty room over a green-grocer's shop in Chelsea and landed on the river-coast of Bohemia. The account of his arrival there in this book is much more vivid and immediate than the description in his *Autobiography*, written in his old age, though no doubt he refreshed his memory of those exciting days by rereading this book, for a great part of it is in fact autobiographical.

It may well have been such a rereading that prompted him in 1950 to suggest, almost timidly, that I might like to reissue *Bohemia in London* under my own imprint, which I had started three years earlier, with David Garnett as one of my partners. Ransome took a great interest in the firm from the beginning, and even invested some money in it. He had been brought up to call men friends by their surnames, and although we had been friends since 1933 he had not yet reached the point of using my Christian name. The three following documents speak for themselves.

9 March 1950 *Rupert Hart-Davis Ltd*
53 Connaught Street
London W 2

My dear Ransome,
When I had reread *Bohemia in London* I gave it to David Garnett and, at the risk of mortally offending you, I am enclosing herewith an unexpurgated copy of his report. I agree almost exactly with what he says. We would be more than happy to republish the book if you so decide, and I am quite certain that it won't lose money. Please let me have a line to say you aren't too annoyed.

Yours ever R. H-D.

BOHEMIA IN LONDON

by Arthur Ransome

I have read every word of this, feeling by turns sentimental and amused; laughing now with and now at the author. For this book was written about the world in which I grew up. I was fifteen when it was published and even then had begun to know the Bohemian side of London fairly well. I knew several of the people mentioned in its pages—Edward Thomas was an intimate friend for one—and I frequented the Hampstead salons which Ransome describes with delightful catty accuracy—that of Sylvia Lynd's mother is recognisable and so is that of Dollie Radford.

It is an odd book—full of genuine feeling and understanding which lapses frequently into rather trashy journalism—no doubt as the author tried to spin it out to the required length. It is a mixture of sensibility and commonsense crossed with immature romanticism. The mixture gives it an odd charm which is all the greater for the 'period' absurdities, such as: 'Even the maddest cigarette-smoking art student' is tamed by marriage. In the event of a reprint it might be wise to omit the chapter called 'A Gypsy Poet' which seems to me very weak and unreal. I think a reprint should have a new introduction by the author discussing how far London has changed—and are there young men who feel like this today? I think the illustrations ought probably to be scrapped.

It is not a book which will add lustre to Ransome's name—it is a young, immature and absurd book. But youth and immaturity have decided charm, and the evocation of the city of my childhood is delightful.

DAVID GARNETT*

10 March 1950

Lowick Hall
Ulverston
Lancs

My dear Hart-Davis,

I was plumb delighted with Garnett's account of *Bohemia*. He is right, of course, in his adjectives . . . immature . . . absurd . . . and I think, too, that he is right when he says that it has an odd charm. I was born in 1884 and that book was published in 1907, when I ought to have been at Oxford being laughed out of my idiocies by other young men instead of frantically writing in order to put porridge in the pot. As you know, I took a very long time growing up and have no illusions about my early spawnings. But there is something likeable about that book, though Garnett is right in thinking there is a lot in it that would be better out. If ever I do reprint it, I'll get going with a scalpel, or rather with a claymore. But not yet.

Garnett is wrong about the pictures. We should have been pickier and choosier. For the pictures are like the book, mixed good and feeble. And though lots of them ought to go, others (like "Fleet Street", showing horse-bus and motor-bus together, and the costumes of the period) help to give the book its proper date.

Some day, perhaps, I'll have at it, but I think that when I start whittling down there'll be nothing left and I'll cut my own fingers in the end.

Anyhow, please say "Thank you" to Garnett. It was good of him to take so much trouble, and I

* Printed here by permission of Mr Richard Garnett.

agree with his criticisms (except of the pictures) and am delighted that, as I do, he finds something to like in its account of those old days when Hampstead seemed an ant-heap of genius.

Yours ever A. R.

Some day, cut down by half, it might make a pleasant *little* book.

There the matter rested.

When Ransome said that he "took a very long time growing up" he was understating the fact, for part of him never grew up at all, and it was the undying child in him that made an immediate appeal to the generations of children who have enjoyed *Swallows and Amazons* and its successors.

Anyhow, here is his first "real book", photographed from the original 1907 edition, pictures and all. A few of the characters can be identified from notes in the author's hand. The poet on page 10 whose first book was issued from a doss-house was W. H. Davies. The Japanese artist on page 49 was Yoshio Markino. The girl on pages 54 f. was the American artist Pamela (Pixie) Colman Smith. The Benns on page 56 were Alphaeus and Peggotty Cole. For more about these last three, see Ransome's *Autobiography*.

There was a second edition, issued in 1912 by a man called Charles Granville, who published as Stephen Swift, but since the firm almost immediately went into liquidation, and Granville was imprisoned for bigamy, it is doubtful whether many copies of that edition ever saw the light.

When I reread the book again the other day, after another thirty-three years, I found the charming parts more charming, and the silly passages more endearing, than I had before. Despite Ransome's misgivings I am sure he would be delighted to see his first "real book" republished by Oxford University Press seventy-six years after it was written, and in time for its author's hundredth birthday.

Rupert Hart-Davis

Marske-in-Swaledale
July 1983

INTRODUCTORY CHAPTER

INTRODUCTORY CHAPTER

WHEN authors are honest to themselves, they admit that their books are failures, in that they are never quite what they wished to make them. A book has a wilful way of its own, as soon as it is fairly started, and somehow has a knack of cheating its writer out of itself and changing into something different. It is usually a reversal of the story of "Beauty and the Beast." The odious beast does not become a prince; but a wonderful, clear, brilliant coloured dream (as all books are before they are written) turns in the very hands of its author into a monster that he does not recognise.

I wanted to write a book that would make real on paper the strange, tense, joyful and despairing, hopeful and sordid life that is lived in London by young artists and writers. I wanted to present life in London as it touches the people who come here, like Whittingtons, to seek the gold of fame on London pavements. They are conscious of the larger life of the town, of the struggling millions earning their weekly wages, of the thousands of the abyss who earn no wages and drift from shelter to shelter till they die; they know that there is a mysterious East End, full of crowded, ill-conditioned life; they know that there is a West End, of fine houses and a more elaborate existence; they have a confused knowledge of the whole, but only a part becomes alive and real, as far as they themselves are concerned. That part is the material of which I hoped to make this book.

There are a dozen flippant, merry treatises on Bohemia in London, that talk of the Savage Club, and the Vagabond dinners, and all the other consciously unconventional things that like to consider themselves Bohemian. But these are not the real things; no young poet or artist fresh to London, with all his hopes unrealised, all his capacity for original living unspent, has anything to do with them. They bear no more vital relation to the Bohemian life that is actually lived than masquerades or fancy dress balls bear to more ordinary existence. Members of the Savage Club, guests of the Vagabonds have either grown out of the life that should be in my book, or else have never lived in it. They are respectable citizens, dine comfortably, sleep in feather-beds, and find hot water waiting for them in the mornings. It is, perhaps, the unreality of their pretences that makes honest outsiders who are disgusted at the imitation, or able to compare them with the inhabitants of the Quartier or Montmartre, say that there is no such thing as Bohemia in London.

But there is; and any one who considers the number of adventurous young people fresh from conventional homes, and consequently ready to live in any way other than that to which they have been accustomed, who come to town with heads more full of poetry than sense, must realise how impossible it is that there should not be. Indeed, it is likely that our Bohemia, certainly in these days, is more real than that of Paris, for the Quartier is so well advertised that it has become fashionable, and Americans who can afford it go there, and almost outnumber the others who cannot afford anything else. Of course, in London too, there are people who are Bohemians for fun; but not so many, because the fun in London is not an organised merriment that any one may enjoy who can pay for it. Visitors to London do not find, as they do in Paris, men waiting about the principal streets, offering themselves as guides to Bohemia. The fun is in the life itself, and not to be had less cheaply than by living it.

I wanted to get into my book, for example, the precarious, haphazard existence of the men who dine in Soho not because it is an unconventional thing to do, but because they cannot usually afford to dine at all, and get better and merrier dinners for their money there than elsewhere, the men who, when less opulent, eat mussels from a street stall without unseemly amusement at the joke of doing so, but as solemnly as you and I eat through our respectable meals, solacing themselves meanwhile with the thought of high ideals that you and I, being better fed, find less real, less insistent.

It was a difficult thing to attempt; if I had simply written from the outside, and announced that oddly dressed artists ate bananas in the streets, that is all that could be said; there is an end of it, the meaning, the essence of the thing is lost, and it becomes nothing but a dull observation of a phenomenon of London life. There was nothing for it but to confess, to write in the first person of my own uncomfortable happy years, and to trust that the hall mark of actual experience would give blood and life, at least to some parts of the picture. Now that would have been very pleasant for me, in spite of the risk that a succession of pictures connected by an ego, should seem a conceited ego exhibiting itself by means of a succession of pictures. But there was another bother; for the life would not have been expressed if there were no suggestion of the older time, the memories of famous artists and writers that contribute to make the poetry of the present. Now it was impossibly ludicrous to be continually flying off from the detailed experience of an insignificant person like myself, to dismiss in a cursory sentence men like Johnson, Hazlitt, or Sir Richard Steele. Separate chapters had to be written on historical Bohemia, giving in as short a space as possible something of the atmosphere of reminiscence belonging to particular localities. There are consequently two separate threads intertwisted through the book, general, historical and descriptive chapters, as impersonal as an egotist could make them, chapters on Chelsea, Fleet Street, Soho and Hampstead, and any number of single incidents and talks about different aspects of Bohemian life—in short, all the hotch-potch that would be likely to come out if a Bohemian were doing his best to let some one else understand his manner of living. A chapter on the old bookstalls will jostle with an account of the Soho coffee-houses. One chapter will be a straightforward narrative of an adventure, another a discussion of the amazing contrast between the country and the town, the life of the Bohemians and the places from which they come. The whole, I had hoped, would give something like an impression of the untidy life itself.

* * * * *

Bohemia is an abominable word, with an air of tinsel and sham, and of suburban daughters who criticise musical comedies seriously, and remind you twice in an afternoon that they are quite unconventional. But the best dictionaries define it as: "(1) A certain small country; (2) The gypsy life; (3) Any disreputable life; (4) The life of writers and painters"—in an order of descent that is really quite pleasant. And on consulting a classic work to find synonyms for a Bohemian, I find the following: "Peregrinator, wanderer, rover, straggler, rambler, bird of passage, gadabout, vagrant, scatterling, landloper, waif and stray, wastrel, loafer, tramp, vagabond, nomad, gypsy, emigrant, and peripatetic somnambulist." If we think of the word in the atmosphere of all those others, it is not so abominable after all, and I cannot find a better.

I suppose Villon is the first remembered Bohemian poet. He had an uncomfortable life and an untidy death. Hunted from tavern to tavern, from place to place, stealing a goose there, killing a man here in a drunken brawl, and swinging from a gibbet in the end, he is a worthy example for the consideration of all young people who wish to follow literature or art without any money in their pockets. But even his fate would not deter them. Indeed, when I was setting out, I even wished to emulate him, and was so foolish as to write to an older friend that I wanted to be such another vagabond as Villon, and work and live in my own free way. The conceit of it, the idiocy—and yet, it is something to remember that you have once felt like that. My friend wrote back to me that of all kinds of bondage, vagabondage was the most cruel and the hardest from which to escape. I believe him now, but *then* I adventured all the same.

Looking from Villon down the centuries, Grub Street seems to be the next important historical fact, a street of mean lodgings where poor hacks wrote rubbish for a pittance, or starved—not a merry place.

And then to the happy time in England, when the greatest English critic, William Hazlitt, could write his best on a dead player of hand fives; when Reynolds, the friend of Keats, could write a sonnet on appearing before his lady with a black eye, "after a casual turn up," and speak of "the great men of this age in poetry, philosophy, or *pugilism*."

Then we think of the Romantics in France. There was the sturdy poet, Petrus Borel, setting up his "Tartars' Camp" in a house in Paris, with its one defiant rule pasted on the door: "All clothing is prohibited." There was Balzac, writing for a fortnight on end without leaving his garret. There was Theophile Gautier, wishing he had been born in the pomp of ancient days, contenting his Grecian instincts by writing *Mademoiselle de Maupin* in six weeks in a big, bare room, with foils and boxing gloves lying always ready for the other Romantics who shared the place with him, and played the Porthos and the Aramis with a noble scorn for the nineteenth century. There was the whole jolly crowd that clapped *Hernani* into fame, and lasted bravely on through Murger's day—Murger, with his *Scènes de la Vie de Bohème*, and his melancholy verdict, "Bohemia is the preface to the Academy, the Hospital, or the Morgue.

And now, to-day, in this London Bohemia

of ours, whose existence is denied by the ignorant, all these different atmospheres are blended into as many colours as the iridescence of a street gutter. Our Villons do not perhaps kill people, but they are not without their tavern brawls. They still live and write poetry in the slums. One of the best books of verse published in recent years was dated from a dosshouse in the Marshalsea. Our Petrus Borels, our Gautiers, sighing still for more free and spacious times, come fresh from Oxford or Cambridge, write funny sonnets lamenting the age of Casanova, and, in a pleasant harmless way, do their best to imitate him. Our Reynoldses are mad over football, and compose verse and prose upon the cricket field. Our Romantics strut the streets in crimson sashes, carry daggers for their own delight, and fence and box and compose extravagant happy tales. Grub Street has broken up into a thousand garrets, but the hacks are still the same. And, as for Murger's young men, as for Collin, as for Schaunard with his hundred ways of obtaining a five franc piece, why I knew one who lived well for a year on three and sixpence of his own money and a handsome borrowing face.

"Where are they all?" you ask. "Where is the Quartier?" It is difficult to give an answer without telling lies. For London is more unwieldy than Paris. It is impossible to draw a map, and say, pointing with a finger, "Here are artists, here romantic poets, here playwrights, here writers of polemic prose." They are scattered over a dozen districts, and mingled all together. There are only a few obvious grouping points. The newspapers, of course, are in Fleet Street, and the writers find that much of their life goes here, in the taverns and coffee-houses round about. The British Museum is in Bloomsbury, and students take lodgings in the old squares and in the narrow streets that run up to the Gray's Inn Road. The Charing Cross Road is full of bookshops where all, when they can afford it, buy. Soho is full of restaurants where all, when they can afford it, dine. And Chelsea, dotted with groups of studios, full of small streets, and cheap lodgings, is alive with artists and writers, and rich with memories of both.

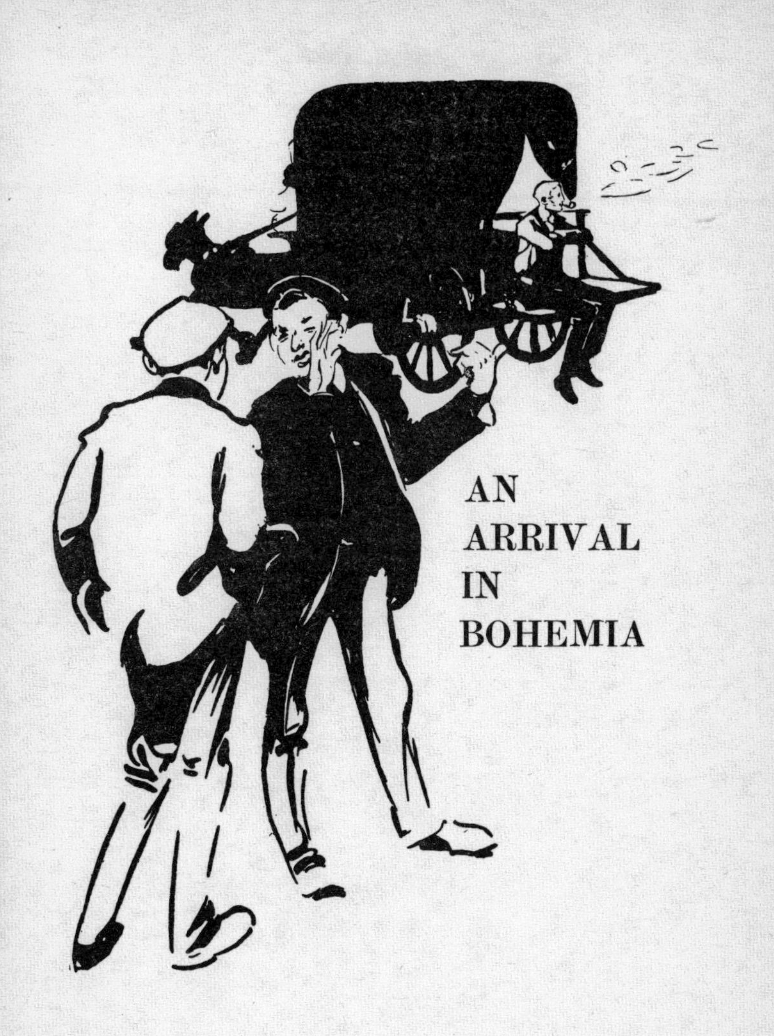

AN ARRIVAL IN BOHEMIA

AN ARRIVAL IN BOHEMIA

I HAD hesitated before coming fairly into Bohemia, and lived for some time in the house of relations a little way out of London, spending all my days in town, often, after a talking party in a Bloomsbury flat or a Fleet Street tavern, missing the last train out at night and being compelled to walk home in the early morning. Would I were as ready for such walks now. Why then, for the sake of one more half hour of laugh and talk and song, the miles of lonely trudge seemed nothing, and all the roads were lit with lamps of poetry and laughter. Down Whitehall I would walk to Westminster, where I would sometimes turn into a little side street in the island of quiet that lies behind the Abbey, and glance at the windows of a house where a poet lived whose works were often in my pocket, to see if the great man were yet abed, and, if the light still glowed behind the blind, to wait a little in the roadway, and dream of the rich talk that might be passing, or picture him at work, or reading, or perhaps turning over the old prints I knew he loved.

Then on, along the Embankment, past the grey mass of the Tate Gallery, past the bridges, looking out over the broad river, now silver speckled in the moonlight, now dark, with bright shafts of light across the water and sparks of red and green from the lanterns on the boats. When a tug, with a train of barges, swept from under a bridge and brought me the invariable, unaccountable shiver with the cold noise of the waters parted by her bows, I would lean on the parapet and watch, and catch a sight of a dark figure silent upon her, and wonder what it would be like to spend all my days eternally passing up and down the river, seeing ships and men, and knowing no hours but the tides, until her lights would vanish round a bend, and leave the river as before, moving on past the still lamps on either side.

I would walk on past Chelsea Bridge, under the trees of Cheyne Walk, thinking, with heart uplifted by the unusual wine, and my own youth, of the great men who had lived there, and wondering if Don Saltero's still knew the ghosts of Addison and Steele—and then I would laugh at myself, and sing a snatch of a song that the evening had brought me, or perhaps be led suddenly to simple matters by the sight of the bright glow of light about the coffee-stall, for whose sake I came this way, instead of crossing the river by Westminster or Vauxhall Bridge.

There is something gypsyish about coffee-stalls, something very delightful. Since those days I have known many: there is one by Kensington Church, where I have often bought a cup of coffee in the morning hours, to drink on the paupers' bench along the railings; there is another by Notting Hill Gate, and another in Sloane Square, where we used to take late suppers after plays at the Court Theatre; but there is none I have loved so well as this small untidy box on the Embankment. That was a joyous night when for the first time the keeper of the stall recognised my face and honoured me with talk as a regular customer. More famous men have seldom made me prouder. It meant something, this vanity of being able to add "Evening, Bill!" to my order for coffee and cake. Coffee and cake cost a penny each and are very good. The coffee is not too hot to drink, and the cake would satisfy an ogre. I used to spend a happy twenty minutes among the loafers by the stall. There were several soldiers sometimes, and one or two untidy women, and, almost every night, a very small very old man with a broad shoulder to him, and a kindly eye. The younger men chaffed him, and the women would laughingly offer to kiss him, but the older men, who knew his history, were gentler, and often paid for his cake and coffee, or gave him the luxury of a hardboiled egg. He had once owned half the boats on the reach, and been a boxer in his day. I believe now that he is dead. There were others too, and one, with long black hair and very large eyes set wide apart, attracted me strangely, as he stood there, laughing and talking scornfully and freely with the rest. One evening he walked over the bridge after leaving the stall, and I, eager to know him, left my coffee untasted, and caught him up, and said something or other, to which he replied. He adjusted his strides to mine, and walked on with me towards Clapham. Presently I told him my name and asked for his. He stopped under a lamp-post and looked at me. "I am an artist," said he, "who does not paint, and a famous man without a name." Then, angry perhaps at my puzzled young face, he swung off without saying good-night into one of the side streets. I have often wondered who and what he was, and have laughed a little sadly to think how characteristic he was of the life I was to learn. How many artists there are who do not paint; how many a man without a name, famous and great within his own four walls. He avoided me after that, and I was too shy ever to question him again.

Often the dawn was in the sky before I left the coffee-stall and crossed the river, and then the grey pale mist with the faint lights in it, and the mysterious ghosts of chimneys and bridges, looming far away, seemed the most beautiful thing in life, one of those promises that are fairer than reality. It was easy to be a poet, gazing into that dream that hung over the river; easy to be a painter, with that delicate picture in my eyes. Sometimes, in the middle of the bridge I choked in my throat, and walked on as fast as I could, with my eyes straight before me, that I might leave it, before spoiling that beautiful vision by another even in a little less perfect.

The rest of the journey lay between red brick houses, duteously asleep; ugly flats, ugly villas, as like to each other as the sheets from a printing press, lined the roads, until my eyes were rested from their ugliness by a mile and a half of green and sparsely wooded common land, sometimes young and almost charming on a dewy morning, sometimes old, ragged and miserable in rain. Then I had to turn once more into the wilderness of brick, through which I passed to the ugliest and most abominable of London's unpleasing suburbs.

I do not know quite what it is that leads artists and writers and others whose lives are not cut to the regular pattern, to leave their homes, or the existences arranged for them by their relations, for a life that is seldom as comfortable, scarcely ever as healthy, and nearly always more precarious. It is difficult not to believe that the varying reasons are one in essence as they are one in effect, but I cannot find fewer than three examples, if all cases are to be illustrated.

There is young Mr. William Hazlitt, after being allowed to spend eight years doing little but walking and thinking, suddenly returns to his childhood's plan of becoming an artist, works like mad, gets a commission to copy

Titians in the Louvre, lives hugger-mugger for four months in Paris, and returns to spend three years tramping the North of England as an itinerant portrait painter. De Quincey, on the other hand, walks out from his school gates, with twelve guineas (ten borrowed) in his pockets, to his adventurous vagabondage on the Welsh hills, for no more urgent reason than that his guardians' ideas do not jump with his in the matter of sending him instantly to college. These are the men marked out early for art or literature. The one sets out because his old ones are not in sufficient subservience to him, the other because they think him a genius and allow him to do what he wants. In both of these cases the essential reason seems to be that when either wants anything he wants it pretty badly. But besides these there are the men who, like Goldsmith, take up an art by accident or necessity in later years, and more often than not are sent into the world because they are failures at home, and given their fifty guineas to clear out by an Uncle Contarine who wishes to relieve his brother's or sister's anxieties rather than those of his nephew.

Things were so a hundred years ago, and they are still the same. I was very young, and mad to be a Villon, hungry to have a life of my own. My wishes told my conscience twenty times a day that my work (my work!) could but ill progress in a house where several bustling lives were vividly lived in directions opposite to my own desires. I think my relations must have been quite as anxious to get rid of me. At last I spent a morning prowling

round Chelsea, and found an empty room with four windows all in good condition, and a water supply two floors below, at a rent of a few shillings a week. I paid for a week in advance and went home, ordering a grocer's van to call after lunch. The van drew up before the door. I announced its meaning, packed all my books into it, a railway rug, a bundle of clothes and my one large chair, said good-bye to my relations, and then, after lighting my clay pipe, and seating myself complacently on the tailboard, gave the order to start. I was as Columbus setting forth to a New World, a gypsy striking his tent for unknown woods; I felt as if I had been a wanderer in a caravan from my childhood as I loosened my coat, opened one or two more buttons in the flannel shirt that I wore open at the neck, and saw the red brick houses slipping slowly away behind me. The pride of it, to be sitting behind a van that I had hired myself; to carry my own belongings to a place of my own choosing; to be absolutely a free man, whose most distant desires seemed instantly attainable. I have never known another afternoon like that.

It was very warm, and the bushes in the tiny suburban gardens were grey with dust, and dust clouds blew up from the road, and circled about the back of the van, and settled on my face and in my nostrils as I broadened my chest and snuffed the air of independence. As we came through the busier thoroughfares, errand boys, and sometimes even loafers, who should have had a greater sympathy with me, jeered at my pipe and my clothes, doubtless encouraged by the boy who sat in front and drove, and was (I am sure of it) carrying on a winking conversation. But I minded them no more than the dust. For was I not now a free Bohemian, on my way to the haunts of Savage, and Goldsmith, and Rossetti, and

Lamb, and Whistler, and Steele, and Carlyle, and all the others whose names and histories I knew far better than their works. No, I will not do myself that injustice; I knew nothing of Carlyle's life, but his "Sartor Resartus" was my Bible; I knew little of Lamb, but I had had "Elia" bound privily in the covers of a school Cæsar, to lessen the tedium of well-hated Latin lessons I remember being called upon to construe, and, with unthinking enjoyment, reciting aloud to an astonished class and master the praises of Roast Pork. I knew the works of these two better than their lives. And Carlyle had lived in Chelsea, whither my grocer's van of happiness was threading the suburban streets, and Lamb had lived in a court only a stone's throw from the office of the little newspaper whose payments for my juvenile essays had helped my ambition to o'erleap the Thames and find a lodging for itself.

Over the Albert Bridge we moved as leisurely as the old horse chose to walk in the August sun, and then a little way to the left, and up to the King's Road, by way of Cheyne Walk and Bramerton Street, past the very house of Carlyle, and so near Leigh Hunt's old home that I could have changed the time of day with him had his kindly ghost been leaning from a window. And I thought of these men as I sat, placid and drunk with pride, on the tail-board of the van. Pipe after pipe I smoked, and the floating blue clouds hung peacefully in the air behind me, like the rings in the water made by a steady oarsman. Their frequency was the only circumstance that betrayed my nervousness.

We turned into the King's Road, that was made to save King Charles's coach horses when he drove to see Nell Gwynne. We followed it to the World's End, where I thought of Congreve's "Love for Love," and having the book with me in the van, glanced, for pleasure, in the black print, though I knew the thing by heart, to the charming scene where Mrs. Frail and Mrs. Foresight banter each other on their indiscretions; you remember: Mrs. Foresight taunts her sister with driving round Covent Garden in a hackney coach, alone, with a man, and adds that it is a reflection on her own fair modesty, whereupon sprightly Mrs. Frail retorts:

"Pooh! here's a clutter, why should it reflect upon you? I don't doubt but that you have thought yourself happy in a hackney coach before now. If I had gone to Knightsbridge, or to Chelsea, or to Spring Gardens, or Barn Elms with a man alone, something might have been said."

"Why, was I ever in any of these places? What do you mean, sister?"

"Was I? What do you mean?"

"You have been at a worse place."

"I at a worse place, and with a man!"

"I suppose you would not go alone to the World's End?"

"The World's End? What, do you mean to banter me?"

"Poor Innocent! You don't know that there is a place called the World's End? I'll swear you can keep your countenance purely; you'd make an admirable player. . . . But look you here, now—Where did you lose this gold bodkin?—Oh, sister, sister!"

"My bodkin?"

"Nay, 'tis yours; look at it."

"Well, if you go to that, where did you find this bodkin? Oh, sister, sister—sister every way."

Was ever a more admirable little scene to read upon the tailboard of a van on a hot summer's day? I made my boy pull up, and go in at the tavern and bring out a couple of pints of ale, old ale, one for me, for once his lord and my own master, and one for him to drink my health in, and the health of William Congreve, who doubtless drank here many years ago, when green fields spread between here and Westminster, and this was a little inn, a naughty little inn, where gay young men brought gay young women to talk private business in the country. I saw them sitting in twos outside the tavern with a bottle of wine before them on a trestle-board, and a pair of glasses, or perhaps one between them, graven with the portrait of a tall ship, or a motto of love and good fellowship.

And then, when the ale was done, we went on, and I forgot old Chelsea, the riverside village in the fields; to think upon how I was to spend the night in this new Chelsea, haunted, it was true, by the ghosts of winebibbers and painters and poets, but, to me who was to live in it, suddenly become as frightening and as solitary as an undiscovered land.

In a street of grey houses we stopped at a corner where an alley turned aside; we stopped at the corner house, which was a greengrocer's shop. Slipping down from the tailboard of the van, I looked up at the desolate, curtainless windows of the top floor that showed where I was to sleep.

The landlord was an observant, uncomfortable wretch, who ran the shop on the ground floor, though in no way qualified for a greengrocer, a calling that demands something more of stoutness and juiciness of nature than ever he could show. He watched with his fingers in the pockets of his lean waistcoat the unloading of my van, without offering to help us, and when my vassal and I had carried the things up into the bare top room, he came impertinently in, and demanded "if this were all I had brought? Where was my furniture? He was for none of your carpet-bag lodgers."

"I am just going out to get my furniture," I replied, and, as if by accident, let him see my one gold piece, while from another pocket I paid the boy the seven shillings agreed upon as the hire of the van, with an extra shilling for himself. He watched unimpressed, till I moved towards the door with such an air that he withdrew with a little more deference, though he chose to descend the stairs before me. I hated him. His manner had almost been a damper on my happiness.

From the nearest grocer's shop I bought three shillings' worth of indifferently clean packing-cases, and paid an extra sixpence to have them taken home at once. I went on along the Fulham Road, buying apples, and cheese, and bread, and beer, till my pockets and arms were laden with as much as they could carry. When I returned, the boxes had been delivered, and my landlord was standing indignant in the middle of my room.

"You must understand——" he began at once.

My temper was up. "I do," I replied. "Have you the key of the door? Thank you. Good night," and smiled happily to myself as the shuffling footsteps of that mean-spirited greengrocer died away down the stairs.

The lodging was a large square place, and did not (I admit it now, though I would have shot myself for the thought then) look very cheerful. Bare and irregular boards made its floor; its walls were dull grey green; my books were piled in a cruelly careless heap in one corner, my purchases in another; the pile of packing cases in the middle made it appear the very lumber room it was.

The boxes were soon arranged into a table and chairs. Two, placed one above the other on their sides, served for a cupboard. Three set end to end made an admirable bed. Indeed my railway rug gave it an air of comfort, even of opulence, spread carefully over the top. The cheese was good, and also the beer, but I had forgotten to buy candles, and it was growing dark before that first untidy supper was finished. So I placed a packing-case chair by the open window, and dipped through a volume of poetry, an anthology of English ballads, that had been marked at ninepence on an open bookstall in the Charing Cross Road.

But I did not read much. The sweet summer air, cool in the evening, seemed to blow a kiss of promise on my forehead. The light was dying. I listened for the hoot of a steamer on the river, or the bells of London churches; I heard with elation the feet of passengers, whom I could see but dimly, beating on the pavement far below. A rough voice was scolding in the room under mine, and some one was singing a song. Now and again I looked at the poetry, though it was really too dark to see, and a thousand hopes and fears flitting across the page carried me out of myself, but not so far that I did not know that this was my first night of freedom, that for the first time in my life I was alone in a room of my own, free to live for poetry, for philosophy, for all the things that seemed then to matter more than life itself. I thought of Crabbe coming to London with three pounds in his pockets, and a volume of poems; I thought of Chatterton, and laughed at myself, but was quite a little pleased at the thought. Brave dreams flooded my mind, and I sat content long after it was dusk and smoked, and sent with infinite enjoyment puffs of pale smoke out into the night. I did not go to bed at all, but fell asleep leaning on the window sill, to wake with a cold in my head.

OLD AND NEW CHELSEA

OLD AND NEW CHELSEA

CHELSEA has waged more than a hundred years' war with the common sense of the multitude. Long before Leigh Hunt settled with his odd household in Upper Cheyne Row, with Carlyle for a neighbour, Chelsea had begun to deserve its reputation as a battle-field and bivouacking ground for art and literature.

Somewhere about 1690 an inventive barber and ex-servant called Salter, who renamed himself Don Saltero, with an eye to trade, set up at No. 18 Cheyne Walk a coffee-house and mad museum. Those who wished for coffee visited the museum, and those who came to view the curiosities—which were many and various, including a wild man of the woods, and the tobacco pipe of the Emperor of Morocco—refreshed their minds with coffee. Some trades seem invented to provide the material of delightful literature ; barbers especially are men whom the pen does but tickle to caress. Don Quixote met such an one in the adventure of the helmet; Shibli Bagarag of Shiraz, the shaver of Shagpat.

the son of Shimpoor, the son of Shoolpi, the son of Shullum, was a second; and Don Saltero seems to have been just such another. Steele wrote a laughing friendly portrait of him in the *Tatler*:—

"When I came into the Coffee House I had no time to salute the Company before my Eye was taken by ten thousand Gimcracks round the Room, and on the Ceiling. When my first astonishment was over comes to me a Sage of a thin and meagre Countenance; which aspect made me doubt whether Reading or Fretting had made him so philosophick. But I very soon perceived him to be of that Sect which the Ancients called Ginquistae; in our Language Tooth Drawers. I immediately had a respect for the man; for these practical philosophers go upon a very rational Hypothesis, not to cure but to take away the Part affected. My Love of Mankind made me very benevolent to Mr. Salter, for such is the name of this Eminent Barber and Antiquary."

Steele was not the only man of letters who loved the place. Doctor Tobias Smollett, when he lived in Chelsea, used to stroll in here of an afternoon. On Sundays he was busy feeding poor authors at his own house on "beef, pudding, and potatoes, port, punch, and Calvert's Entire butt-beer," but on week days he went often to Don Saltero's, where he may have seen Benjamin Franklin, a journeyman printer dutifully examining the place as one of the London sights. Indeed, against the inexcusable autobiography of that austere, correct fellow we must set the fact of his swim back from Chelsea down to Blackfriars. We can forgive him much righteousness for that. But Steele's is the pleasantest memory of the old museum. I think of the meagre barber, proud of his literary patrons, serving coffee to them in the room decorated with gimcracks on ceiling, walls, and floor; but I should have loved above all to see Steele swing in, carelessly dressed, with his whole face smiling as he showed Mr. Salter his little advertisement in the lazy pages of the *Tatler*, fresh and damp from the press.

Though No. 18 has long been a private house, Chelsea still knows such characters as the man who made it famous. I lost sight of one of them only a year or two ago. I forget his name, but he called himself the "P.B." which letters stood for "The Perfect Bohemian." He wrote most abominable bad verses, and kept a snug little restaurant in the Fulham Road, a happy little feeding house after the old style, now, alas! fallen into a more sedate proprietorship. Half a dozen of us used to go there at one time, and drank coffee, and ate fruit stewed by the poet himself. We sat on summer evenings in a small partly roofed yard behind the house. Creepers hung long trails with fluttering leaves over green painted tables, and, as dark came on, the P.B. would light Japanese lanterns that swung among the foliage, and then, sitting on a table, would read his poetry aloud to his customers. The restaurant did not pay better than was to be expected, and the P.B. became an artist's model. He was fine-looking, with curly hair, dark eyes, a high brow, and the same meagreness about his face that Steele noticed in the ingenious barber. I hope he made a fortune as a model. He must have been an entertaining sitter.

I had been looking for a picture of old irregular family life when I came on Carlyle's description of the Hunts. It is curious how slowly Bohemia changes. The last fifty years, that have altered almost everything else, have left the little Bohemian family life that there is very like this, at any rate in essentials :

"Hunt's household. Nondescript! Unutterable! Mrs. Hunt asleep on cushions; four or five beautiful, strange, gypsy-looking children running about in undress, whom the lady ordered to get us tea. The eldest boy, Percy—a sallow black-haired youth of sixteen, with a kind of dark cotton nightgown on—went whirling about like a familiar, pervading everything; an indescribable dreamlike household. . . . Hunt's house excels all you have ever heard of . . . a poetical Tinkerdom, without parallel even in literature. In his family room, where are a sickly large wife and a whole school of well-conditioned wild children, you will find half a dozen old rickety chairs gathered from half a dozen different hucksters, and all seeming engaged, and just pausing, in a violent hornpipe. On these and round them and over the dusty table and ragged carpets lie all kinds of litter—books, paper, eggshells and, last night when I was there, the torn half of a half-quartern loaf. His own room above stairs, into which alone I strive to enter, he keeps cleaner. It has only two chairs, a book-case and a writing table; yet the noble Hunt receives you in his Tinkerdom in the spirit of a King, apologises for nothing, places you in the best seat, takes a window-sill himself if there is no other, and then, folding closer his loose flowing "muslin cloud" of a printed nightgown, in which he always writes, commences the liveliest dialogue on philosophy and the prospects of man (who is to be beyond measure happy yet), which again he will courteously terminate the moment you are bound to go."

As for Carlyle's own house, just round the corner, he left a description of that too, in a letter to his wife, written to her when he took it.

". . . on the whole a most massive, roomy, sufficient old house, with places, for example, to hang, say, three dozen hats or cloaks on, and as many curious and queer old presses and shelved closets (all tight and well painted in their way) as would satisfy the most covetous Goody: rent thirty-five pounds. . . . We lie safe at a bend of the river, away from all the great roads, have air and quiet hardly inferior to Craigenputtock, an outlook from the back windows into more leafy regions, with here and there a red high-peaked old roof looking through, and see nothing of London except by day the summits of St. Paul's Cathedral and Westminster Abbey, and by night the gleam of the great Babylon, affronting the peaceful skies. The house itself is probably the best we have ever lived in—a right old strong roomy brick house built nearly one hundred and fifty years ago, and likely to see three races of these modern fashionables come down."

There it stands still, and in a way to fulfil the prophecy. The houses have closed in about its quiet street. The little villagery of Chelsea has been engulfed in the lava stream of new cheap buildings. The King's Road thunders with motor buses and steam vans, but here in this quiet Cheyne Row the sun yet falls as peacefully as ever on the row of trees along the pavement, and, over the way, on the stiff front of the "sufficient old house," in at the windows where Carlyle sat and smoked long pipes with Tennyson, and talked to "my old friend Fitzgerald, who might have spent his time to much better purpose than in busying himself with the verses of that old Mahometan blackguard," Omar Khayyam. They tell me that upstairs is still the double-walled room where so many groans were hurled at unnecessary noises and the evils of digestion, and where, in spite of all, so many great books came alive on the paper. There is a medallion on the front of the house, and visitors are allowed to nose about inside. But it is better to forget the visitors, as you look down that shady street on a summer's day, and to think only of the old poet-philosopher who was so happy there and so miserable, and loved so well the river that flows statelily past the foot of the street. There, looking out over the water, from the narrow gardens along Cheyne Walk, you may see his statue, the patron saint of so many wilfully bad-tempered fellows, who cannot, as he could, vindicate their bad temper by their genius.

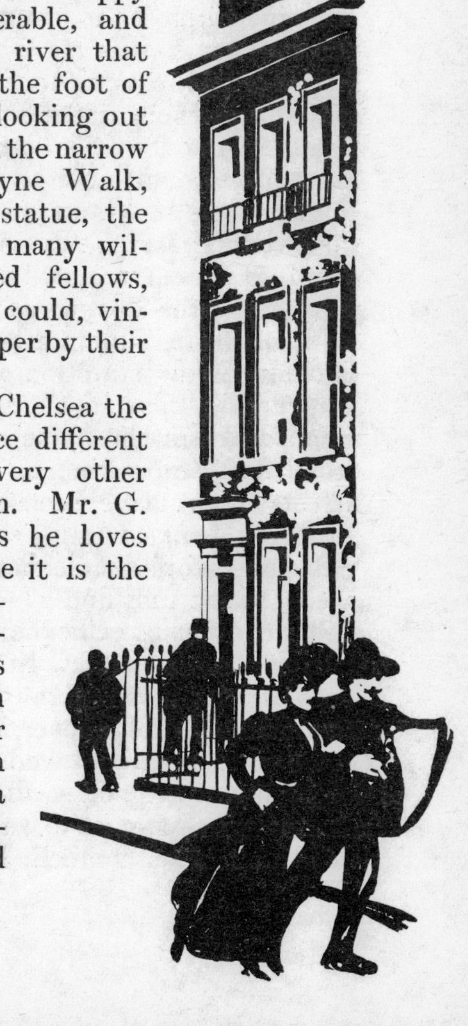

The river made Chelsea the place it is, a place different specially from every other suburb of the town. Mr. G. K. Chesterton says he loves Battersea, "because it is the only suburb that retains a local patriotism." Chelsea has a local patriotism too, but of another kind, the patriotism of members of a foreign legion. Chelsea does not breed artists, she adopts them; but they would die for her. But apart from this patriotism, she has a local atmosphere that has nothing to do with the artists, the feeling of a riverside village that not even the rival highway of the King's Road has been able to destroy. Chelsea was once such a place for Londoners as Chertsey is now. People came there to be near the river. Visitors to the World's End, then the limit of fashion, where gallants brought their Mrs. Frails, came by boat. Big country houses were built round about. Sir Thomas More's house, where he entertained Holbein and the observant Erasmus, was built in 1521 where Beaufort Street is now, and had "a pleasant prospect of the Thames and the fields beyond." And all the best memories of old Chelsea rest in the narrow stately fronted houses along Cheyne Walk, or in the little taverns by the riverside, or in the narrow streets that run up from the Embankment, just as the village streets might have been expected to run up from the banks of the stream when, in the old days, people came here to bathe and be merry in the sunshine.

Three of those Cheyne Walk houses must be mentioned here. In 1849 some members of the newly-established Pre-Raphaelite Brotherhood looked over No. 16, "with which they were greatly taken. It is capable of furnishing four good studios, with a bedroom, and a little room that would do for a library, attached to each. 'P. R. B.' might be written on the door, and stand for 'Please Ring the Bell' to the profane. . . ." How cheerful that is. But the house was not taken till a dozen years afterwards, when Rossetti, whose life had been broken by the death of his wife nine months before, took it with Swinburne and Meredith. In the back garden he kept all manner of strange beasts, zebus, armadillos, and the favourite of all, the wombat, an animal almost canonised by the Pre-Raphaelites. "Do you know the wombat at the Zoo?" asked Rossetti, before he had one of his own, "a delightful creature, the most comical little beast." They used in the early days to make pilgrimages to Regent's Park on purpose to see it, and in Lady Burne-Jones's life of her husband she records how the windows in the Union at Oxford, whitened while Morris and Rossetti and the rest were decorating, were covered with sketches of wombats in delightful poses. I wish I could get a picture of one to make a jolly island in the text of this book.

Going west along Cheyne Walk, past Oakley Street and the statue of Carlyle, past old Chelsea Church, we come to Whistler's lofty studio-house, a grey magnificence of which it is impossible to tire. Here lived Whistler in his own way, and flaunted his own way of living. He had some sport with his life. There is a tale told of him before he lived here, when he had the White House in Tite Street, that is very pertinent to this book, and is the more interesting in that it is the duplicate of one of Sir Richard Steele's exploits. Mr. William Rossetti gives the story in his big book of reminiscences, and Johnson in almost the same terms tells the same tale of Steele, who is known to have rented a house somewhere along the waterside. Here is the Steele story; the Whistler is exactly similar, but I have not the book in the house:

"Sir Richard Steele one day having invited to his house a great number of persons of the first quality, they were surprised at the number of liveries which surrounded the table; and after dinner, when wine and mirth had set them free from the observations of a rigid ceremony, one of them inquired of Sir Richard how such an expensive train of domestics could be consistent with his fortunes. Sir Richard very frankly confessed that they were fellows of whom he would willingly be rid. And then, being asked why he did not discharge them, declared that they were bailiffs, who had introduced themselves with an execution, and whom, since he could not send them away, he had thought it convenient to embellish with liveries, that they might do him credit while they stayed."

Johnson does not say whether it was in Chelsea that this occurred. So it is safer, and at least as pleasant, to read Whistler for Steele, and imagine the dinner party in Tite Street. The humour of it would have delighted either of these very different men. Whistler must have carried it off with a superb nicety, but it is not told that his friends paid up, and set him free, as they did for Dick Steele. It is possible he would have resented it.

Further along Cheyne Walk, beyond Battersea Bridge, where the stately houses dwindle into a regular little riverside street, with cottages, and nondescript shops, and nautical taverns, with old quays and landing stairs just over the way, is No. 118, a tiny red-tiled house, a little below the level of the street, set back between an inn and a larger house, behind faded wooden palings, and a few shrubs. There are birds' nests in the creepers that cover the walls and twist about the windows. Here Turner lived under an assumed name (they thought him an old sea captain) and climbed the roof to watch the sunsets, as a retired sailor might watch for small shipping coming down the river. Here he died in 1851, a tired old man, only a few years after Ruskin had proved to the world that of all modern painters he was the greatest and least honoured.

Now, in the twentieth century, the riverside streets only live their old lives in the minds of the young and unsuccessful who walk their pavements in the summer evenings. Those who rent houses in Tite Street or in Cheyne Walk live nicely and reverently.

They are either more respectable than Steele or Whistler, or less magnificent. Bohemia has moved a little further from the river. The river has given place to the King's Road as Chelsea's main artery, and now the old exuberant life is lived, not in the solemn beautiful houses by the waterside, nor in the taverns by the deserted quays, but in the studios and squares and narrow streets along the other thoroughfare. There is Glebe Place, full of studios; there is Bramerton Street, and Flood Street, and then there is modern Chelsea, a long strip of buildings cut by narrow streets, between the King's Road and the Fulham Road. Studios are dotted all about, and at least half the ugly, lovable little houses keep a notice of "Apartments to Let" permanently in the windows, an apt emblem of the continual flitting that is characteristic of the life.

But there is a time in the evening when the irregulars of these days cross the King's Road and usurp the Bohemia of the past. When it grows too dark for painters to judge the colours of their pictures, they flock out from the studios, some to go up to Soho for dinner, some to stroll with wife or friendly model in the dusk. The favourite promenade is along Cheyne Walk, where the lamps shining among the leaves of the trees cast wavering shadows on the pavements. Only the black-and-white men, working against time for the weekly papers, plug on through the dark.

Now and again, walking the streets, you may look up at a window and see a man busily drawing, with a shaded lamp throwing a bright light on the Bristol-board before him. For myself, I soon discovered that the dusk was meant for indolence, and always, a little before sunset, threaded my way to the King's Road, and so to the river. I would leave the spider strength of the Albert Bridge behind me, and stroll on past Battersea Bridge to a promontory of embankment just beyond, the best of all places for seeing the sunsets up the river, and the blue mists about those four tall chimneys of the electric generating station. I used to lean on the balustrade there and watch the green and golden glow fade away from the sky where those great obelisks towered up, and think of Turner on the roof of the little house close by; I would watch the small boats bobbing on their ropes, and listen for the noises of the King's Road behind the buildings to the right, or the clangour of the factories on the other side of the water. And then I would turn, and watch the butterflies of fire flash out of the dusk and perch along the bridge in glittering clusters. As the dark fell, lights shone out along the Embankment, climbed slowly up the rigging of the boats by the wharf, and lit up the square windows of the houses and taverns by the waterside. Often, walking along, when the reflections followed me with long indexes across the water as I moved, when the tugs coming round the bend of the river lit up their red and green, when over everything hung that mist so miraculously blue that it took a Whistler to perceive it, I have thought of the old times when kings and philosophers bathed in the reeds here, and when at night there were no lights at all, except where the sailors were merry in a tavern, or a Steele was giving a party in one of the big houses. I have thought of Chelsea and her river in those days, and Chelsea and her river in ours, and then, as I have looked again along the glimmering Embankment, or seen a poet and a girl pass by arm-in-arm, with eyes wide open to that spangled loveliness that smiles undaunted by the stars, I have thought it not impossible that we are the more fortunate in knowing Chelsea now.

A CHELSEA EVENING

A CHELSEA EVENING

CHELSEA seemed, in spite of all its memories, a desolate lonely place when I woke sitting on the packing case by the window of my lodging on the morning after my arrival. It became populous with friends, through circumstances so typical of the snowball growth of acquaintanceship, and of one kind of Chelsea life, that they deserve a description in detail.

The only man I knew in Chelsea was a Japanese artist who had been my friend in even earlier days, when both he and I had been too poor to buy tobacco. We had known each other pretty well, and he had come to Chelsea some months before. I called on him, and found him lodging in a house where he shared a sitting-room with an actor. This man, called Wilton, was such an actor that he seemed a very caricature of his own species. It was a delight to watch him. He was lying at full length on a dilapidated sofa, so arranged that he could, without moving, see his face in a mirror on the other side of the room. He was very long, and in very long fingers he held a cigarette. Sometimes, with the other hand, he would rumple the thick black hair over his forehead, and then he would open his eyes as wide as he could, and glance with satisfaction towards the looking-glass. The Japanese, twinkling with mirth, was seated straddlewise round the back of a chair by the fireplace, and was trying eagerly, with short flashes of uncertain English, to reason the actor into a piece of common sense about his profession. He jumped up when I came in, and the actor languidly introduced himself. Then they continued the discussion. Wilton refused to believe that observation was in any way necessary to his art.

"Pluck," he said, with a magnificent gesture, "your characters from your own heart and soul. If I act a king, I will be a king in my own right, and find all majesty and pride in my own consciousness."

I thought privily that he might find that easy, but the Japanese, reasoning more seriously, continued: "But if you were going to act an idiot or a drunkard, would not you——?"

"No, I would not. Every man, or all great men, have all possibilities within them. I could be divinely mad without ever wasting time in watching the antics of a madman."

"But do you tell us you would dare to act the drunkard, without watching to see how he walks, and how he talks, and sings? Would you act an old woman and get true like, without seeing first an old woman to copy the mumbling of her lips?"

"Ah," said the actor, with delighted logic, "but I would never act an old woman. And you are losing your temper, my dear fellow. Some day, when you consider the matter more calmly, you will realise that I am right. But do not let men of genius quarrel over an argument."

And then, as the Japanese smiled unperceived at me, and rolled a cigarette, the superb Wilton turned himself a little on the sofa, rearranged a cushion beneath his elbow, and began a long half-intoned speech about newspapers, the folly of reading them, the inconceivable idiocy of those who write for them, and so forth, while I agreed with him at every point, and the Japanese, who knew my means of livelihood, chuckled quietly to himself.

The actor was happy. Flattered by my continual agreement, the billows of his argument rolled on and broke with increasing din along the shores of silence. The only other sound beside the long roll of his impassioned dogma was the low murmur of my assent. Give a fool a proselyte, and he will be ten times happier than a sage without one. Wilton must have enjoyed that afternoon. He thought he had a proselyte in me, and he talked like a prophet, till I wondered how it could be possible for any one man's brain to invent such floods of nonsense. I was happy under it all, if only on account of the quiet quizzical smile of the Japanese, who was making a sketch of the orator's face.

The end of it was that he fell in love with an audience so silent, so appreciative, and decided that he must really have me with him that night, at the house of a lady who once a week gave an open party for her friends. I was wanted, it was clear, as a foil to his brilliance. It was at least an adventure, and I agreed to come. What was the lady's name, I asked, and what was she?

He was too impatient to go on with his harangue to tell me anything except that she was an artist, and that at her rooms I would meet the best poets and painters and men and women of spirit in the town. "Indeed," he added, "I go there myself, regularly, once a week."

A red-haired serving maid brought up tea at this moment, before he had again got fairly into the swing of his discourse, and he withheld his oratory to give directions for us, as to the quantities of milk and sugar we should mix for him, together with a little general information on the best methods of drinking tea. The Japanese set a chair by the sofa for him, and I carried him his cup and saucer, and a plate of bread and butter from the table. He ate and drank in silence for a moment, and then broke out again in florid talk about slavery on sugar plantations, the text being the two lumps which, at his orders, had been placed in his saucer. After tea, he went on talking, talking, talking, until eight in the evening, when he went upstairs to put on a clean collar and to rearrange his hair.

Presently he reappeared, with a curl above his forehead. He suggested that we should start. The Japanese excused himself from accompanying us, and went down to the river to make studies for some painting upon which he was engaged. We set off together down the Fulham Road, in the most beautiful light of a summer evening. There was a glow in the sky that was broken by the tall houses, and the tower of the workhouse lifted bravely up into the sunset. Below, in the blue shadows of the street, people were moving, and some of the shops had lights in them. It was a perfect night, and completely wasted on the actor, and indeed on me too, for I was intent on observing him. Now and again, as he strode along the pavement, a girl would turn to look at his tall figure, and it was plain that he noticed each such incident with pleasure. When we came among the shops, he would now and again do his best to catch sight of himself in the glasses of the windows, and occasionally, to this end, would stop with a careless air, and light a cigarette, or roll one, or throw one away into the road. The whole world was a pageant to him, with himself a central figure.

At last we turned to the right, between houses with narrow gardens and little trees in front of them, and then to the right again, till we stopped at the end of a short street. "Her name is Gypsy," he said dramatically. "No one ever calls her anything else." Then he swung open the garden gate, walked up the steps of the house, and knocked vigorously on the door. Through a window on the left I had caught a glimpse of a silver lamp, and a brazen candlestick, and a weird room in shaded lamplight. I was tiptoe with excitement. For I was very young.

Some one broke off in a song inside, and quick steps shuffled in the passage. The door was flung open, and we saw a little round woman, scarcely more than a girl, standing in the threshold. She looked as if she had been the same age all her life, and would be so to the end. She was dressed in an orange-coloured coat that hung loose over a green skirt, with black tassels sewn all over the orange silk, like the frills on a red Indian's trousers. She welcomed us with a little shriek. It was the oddest, most uncanny little shriek, half laugh, half exclamation. It made me very shy. It was obviously an affectation, and yet seemed just the right manner of welcome from the strange little creature, "goddaughter of a witch and sister to a fairy," who uttered it. She was very dark, and not thin, and when she smiled, with a smile that was peculiarly infectious, her twinkling gypsy eyes seemed to vanish altogether. Just now at the door they were the eyes of a joyous excited child meeting the guests of a birthday party.

The actor shook hands, and, in his annoying laughable dramatic manner, introduced me as "a clever young man who has read philosophy." I could have kicked him.

"Come in!" she cried, and went shuffling down the passage in that heavy parti-coloured dress.

We left our hats and followed her into a mad room out of a fairy tale. As soon as I saw it I knew she could live in no other. It had been made of two smaller chambers by the removal of the partition wall, and had the effect of a well-designed curiosity shop, a place that Gautier would have loved to describe. The walls were dark green, and covered with brilliant coloured drawings, etchings and pastel sketches. A large round table stood near the window, spread with bottles of painting inks with differently tinted stoppers, china toys, paperweights of odd designs, ashtrays, cigarette boxes, and books; it was lit up by a silver lamp, and there was an urn in the middle of it, in which incense was burning. A woolly monkey perched ridiculously on a pile of portfolios, and grinned at the cast of a woman's head, that stood smiling austerely on the top of a black cupboard, in a medley of Eastern pottery and Indian gods. The mantel-shelves, three stories high, were laden with gimcracks. A low bookcase, crammed and piled with books, was half hidden under a drift of loose pieces of music. An old grand piano, on which two brass bedroom candlesticks were burning, ran back into the inner room, where in the darkness was a tall mirror, a heap of crimson silks, and a low table with another candle flickering among the bottles and glasses on a tray. Chairs and stools were crowded everywhere, and on a big blue sofa against the wall a broadly whiskered picture dealer was sitting, looking at a book of Japanese prints.

We had scarcely been introduced to him, and settled into chairs, while the little woman in the orange coat was seating herself on a cushion, when a quick tap sounded on the window-pane. "The Birds," she cried, and ran back into the passage. A moment or two later she came back, and a pair of tiny artists, for all the world like happy sparrows, skipped into the room. The actor knew them, and welcomed them in his magnificent way. They were the Benns, and had but recently married; she modelled in clay and wax, and he was a painter newly come from Paris. Two people better deserving their nickname would be hard to find. They flitted about the place, looking at the new prints hung on the walls, at the new china toy that Gypsy had been unable to deny herself, and chattering all the time. Benn and I were soon friendly, and he presently asked me to visit his studio. Just as he gave me a card with his address upon it, for which he had to ask his wife, he was caught by a sudden remembrance, and turning about asked Gypsy pointblank across the broadside of conversation, "I say, you haven't such a thing as a big sword, have you?" Oh yes, but she had, and in a minute the two little people were looking at a gigantic two-edged sword, as long as either of them, that hung from a hook on the wall. The actor, with a delighted exhibition of grace and height, reached it easily down, and Benn was for swinging it at once, with all the strength that he had, if his wife had not instantly brought him to sense and saved the place from devastation. Instead, he described the picture he was painting. The central figure, he told us, was to be an old knight looking regretfully at the armour and weapons he had used in his youth. This was the very sword for his purpose.

Just then there was another tap, and two women came in together. The first was a tall dark Scottish girl, with a small head and a beautiful graceful neck, very straight and splendid (I called her the Princess at once in my fantastic boyhood), and the other a plump jolly American.

As soon as the shaking of hands was all over, some one asked Gypsy for a song. "Got very little voice to-night," she coughed, "and everybody wants something to drink first. But I'll sing you a song afterwards." She went through to the table with the glasses in the inner room. "Who is for opal hush?" she cried, and all, except the American girl and the picture dealer, who preferred whisky, declared their throats were dry for nothing else. Wondering what the strange-named drink might be, I too asked for opal hush, and she read the puzzlement in my face. "You make it like this," she said, and squirted lemonade from a syphon into a glass of red claret, so that a beautiful amethystine foam rose shimmering to the brim. "The Irish poets over in Dublin called it so; and once, so they say, they went all round the town, and asked at every public-house for two tall cymbals and an opal hush. They did not get what they wanted very easily, and I do not know what a tall cymbal may be. But this is the opal hush." It was very good, and as I drank I thought of those Irish poets, whose verses had meant much to me, and sipped the stuff with reverence as if it had been nectar from Olympus.

When everybody had their glasses, Gypsy came back into the front part of the room, and, sitting in a high-backed chair that was covered with gold and purple embroideries, she cleared her throat, leant forward so that the lamplight fell on her weird little face, and sang, to my surprise, the old melody:

"O the googoo bird is a giddy bird,
No other is zo gay.
O the googoo bird is a merry bird,
Her zingeth all day.
Her zooketh zweet flowers
To make her voice clear,
And when her cryeth googoo, googoo,
The zummer draweth near."

Somehow I had expected something else. It

seemed odd to hear that simple song drop word by word in the incense-laden atmosphere of that fantastic room.

After that she chanted in a monotone one of the poems from Mr. Yeats's "Wind Among the Reeds":

> "I went out into the hazel wood,
> Because a fire was in my head,
> And cut and peeled a hazel wand,
> And hooked a berry to a thread."
>
> . . . .
>
> . . . .

And then the stately Scottish girl sat down at the old piano, and after playing an indolent little melody over the faded yellow keys, brought out in tinkling sweetness the best of all the songs that have ever come to London from the sea. Nearly all the company knew it by heart and sang together:

> "Farewell and adieu to you, fair Spanish ladies,
> Adieu and farewell to you, ladies of Spain;
> For we've received orders for to sail for Old England,
> And we may never see you, fair ladies, again.
>
> "So we'll rant and we'll roar, like true British sailors,
> We'll range and we'll roam over all the salt seas,
> Until we strike anchor in the channel of Old England;
> From Ushant to Scilly 'tis thirty-five leagues."

It is no wonder that such a lad as I was then should find the scene quite unforgettable. There was the beautiful head of the pianist, swaying a little with her music, and the weird group beside her—Gypsy in the orange coat leaning over her shoulder, the two small artists, on tiptoe, bending forward to remind themselves of the words, the hairy picture-dealer smiling on them benignantly, the actor posing against the mantelpiece, the plump American leaning forward with her elbows on the table, her chin in her hands, a cigarette between her lips, with the background of that uncanny room, with the silver lamp, the tall column of smoke from the incense urn, and the mad colours, that seemed, like the discordant company, to harmonise perfectly in those magical surroundings.

When the song was done, the actor told me how its melody had been taken down from an old sailor in this very room. The old fellow, brought here for the purpose, had been shy, as well he might be, and his mouth screwed into wrinkles so that no music would come from it. At last they made him comfortable on a chair, with a glass and a pipe, and built a row of screens all round him, that he might not be shamed. After a minute or two, when the smoke, rising in regular puffs above the screens told them that he had regained his peace of mind, some one said, "Now, then!" and a trembling whistling of the tune had given a musician the opportunity to catch the ancient melody on the keyboard of the piano. They had thus the pride of a version of their own, for they did not know until much later that another had already been printed in a song-book.

Presently the American girl begged for a story. Gypsy had spent some part of her life in the Indies, and knew a number of the old folk tales, of Annansee the spider, another Brer Rabbit in his cunning and shrewdness, and Chim Chim the little bird, and the singing turtle, and the Obeah Woman, who was a witch, "wid wrinkles deep as ditches on her brown face." She told them in the old dialect, in a manner of her own. Fastening a strip of ruddy tow about her head, so that it mingled with her own black hair, she flopped down on the floor, behind a couple of lighted candles, and, after a little introductory song that she had learned from a Jamaican nurse, told story after story, illustrating them with the help of wooden toys that she had made herself. She told them with such precision of phrasing that those who came often to listen soon had them by heart, and would interrupt her like children when, in a single word, she went astray. To hear her was to be carried back to the primitive days of story-telling, and to understand, a little, how it was that the stories of the old minstrels were handed on from man to man with so little change upon the way.

That was my first evening of friendliness in Chelsea. For a long time after that I never let a week pass without going to that strange room to listen to the songs and tales, and to see the odd parties of poets and painters, actors and actresses, and nondescript irregulars who were there almost as regularly as I. Sometimes there would be half a dozen of us, sometimes twenty. Always we were merry. The evening was never wasted. There I heard poetry read as if the ghost of some old minstrel had descended on the reader, and shown how the words should be chanted aloud. There I heard stories told that were yet unwritten, and talk that was so good that it seemed a pity that it never would be. There I joined in gay jousts of caricature. There was a visitors' book that we filled with drawings and rhymes. Every evening that we met we used its pages as a tournament field,

> "And mischievous and bold were the strokes we gave,
> And merrily were they received."

There, too, we used to bring our work when we were busy upon some new thing, a painting, or a book, and work on with fresh ardour after cheers or criticism.

The party broke up on that first night soon after the stories. We helped Gypsy to shut up the rooms and dowse the lights, and waved our good-nights to her as we saw her disappear into the house next door where she lodged.

At the corner of the street the Benns and I were alone, to walk the same way. We went down the Fulham Road together, those two small people chattering of the new picture, and I, swinging the great sword that was to pose for it, walking by the side of them, rejoicing in my new life and in the weight and balance of the sword, a little pleased, boy that I was, to be so much bigger than they, and wondering whether, if I swung the sword with sufficient violence, I had the slightest chance of being rebuked by a policeman for carrying a drawn weapon in the streets.

IN THE STUDIOS

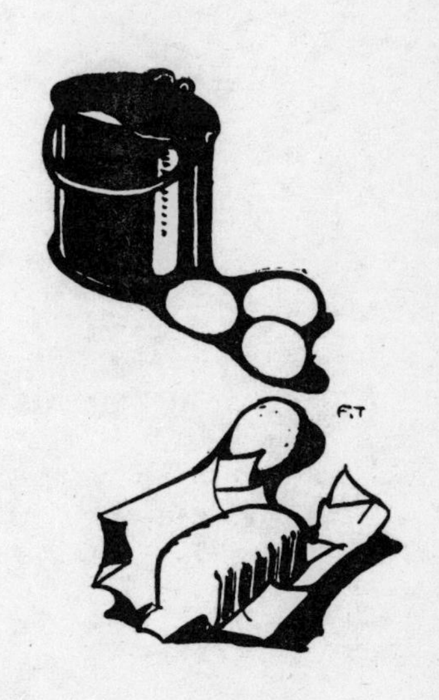

IN THE STUDIOS

A LARGE bare room, with no furniture but a divan or a camp-bed, a couple of chairs, an easel, and a model-stand made of a big box that holds a few coats and hats and coloured silks that do duty in a dozen pictures; a big window slanting up across the roof, with blinds to temper its light; canvases and old paintings without frames leaning against the walls; the artist, his coat off ready for work, strolling up and down with a cigarette between his lips, looking critically and lovingly at the canvas on the easel, and now and again pulling out his watch: that is a fair picture of a studio at about half-past ten on a workaday morning.

There is a tap on the door.

"Come in!" and a girl slips into the room, apologises for the thousandth time in her life for being so late, and proceeds to change her clothes for the costume that will make her the subject he wants for his picture, and then, taking the chair on the top of the costume-box, assumes the pose in which she yesterday began to sit. While she has been getting ready, he has made his last preparations, and turned the key in the door, so that no chance outsider may stumble in and discompose his model.

He looks at his rough drawing, and then at the girl. "We'll get to work now—Your arm was hanging a little further back—Yes—And your head is not quite—That's better—So—Are you easy? We had it natural yesterday —"

"How is this?" She alters herself slightly, and the artist steps back to have another look in order to arrange the drapery.

"There's only one thing wrong now," he will say. "We must just get that dark shadow that there was below your knee."

The girl twists her skirt over, so that it falls in a crease, and gives the streak of dark that he had missed.

"That's it. Well done, Serafina!" he exclaims, and is instantly at work. He has already arranged the blinds over the window so that the light is as it was when he began the painting.

As he paints he tries to keep up some kind of conversation with the girl, so that her mind may be alive, and not allow her to go rigid like a lay figure.

"You are giving me the whole day?" he will ask, although the matter has been settled already.

Gradually, as he grows absorbed in the painting, he has even less brain to spare, and the talk becomes more and more mechanical; but if Serafina is the right kind of model she will do her share of keeping herself amused.

"What have you got for lunch?" she asks.

"Four eggs!"

"What way shall we cook them do you think?"

"You know how to scramble them. Four eggs are enough for that?"

"Yes. I'll scramble them—you have milk?—and butter?"

"Got them first thing this morning. By the way, I met Martin at breakfast. You've posed for him, haven't you?"

And so the talk goes on, like the talk of puppets, she just passing the time, trying to keep interested and real without moving out of her pose; he slashing in the rough work, bringing head, neck, shoulders, the turn of the waist, the fold of the skirt, into their places on the canvas. Then he begins to paint in the details, and is able to tell her what he is about.

"I've done with the right arm for the present. Busy with the face," he says, and she is able to move her arm with relief, and bend it to and fro if it is getting cramped.

It is far more tiring than you would think to remain motionless in a particular pose. The model stiffens insensibly, so that an interval of rest is as necessary for the success of the painting as it is for her own comfort. For a minute or two she will be luxurious in leaving her pose, and he will walk anxiously up and down, looking at the picture, seeking faults, and plotting what to do next with it. And then, with less trouble than at first, she will take her pose again, and he will paint on, and talk emptiness as before.

At last his wrist begins to tire, and he glances at his watch.

"We'll have lunch now. I expect you are ready for it too." He puts down brush and palette, and flings himself on a divan opposite the easel, where he can see the picture. For he works on at it in his head, even when he is not painting. She slips down from the model-stand and puts a match to the little oil stove on the soap box in the corner, takes the eggs and milk and butter out of the cupboard, and sets about making *œufs brouillés*, the favourite dish of half the studios in the world.

Then she will come and look at the picture, and tell him how well and rapidly it is coming together, and what a nice splash of colour the crimson silk gives where the light falls on it. They will sit down to lunch if there is a table, or if not, will walk about the room, eating the eggs with spoons out of saucers, and munching bread and butter. The kettle will be boiling briskly on the stove, and they will make a little brew of coffee, and take a quarter of an hour of leisure, with cigarettes and coffee-cups, before going on with the work.

They are lucky if they can work on long after four o'clock without another knock sounding at the door. There are as many again lazy fellows who go about to waste time as there are hard-working artists. Surely enough, when the picture is all juicy and pliable, when all is going as a painter loves it best, there will come a tap at the locked door.

"Oh, curse!" says the artist under his breath, and paints on, pretending not to hear. Tap comes the knock again. He flings down his brushes, turns the key, and opens the door to the interrupter, one of those pleasant, friendly people who never seem to have anything to do. "Oh, it's you, is it?" he says, as graciously as he can. "Come in."

The man, genial, full of chatter, as they all are, comes in, volubly apologetic. "Look here," he says, "don't let me disturb your work. Oh, hullo! How are you, Serafina? He's doing well with you this time. You'll be in all the papers, my dear, and then you'll be too proud to pose for any but swells. Yes, I'll have a cigarette; and now, look here, don't stop working on my account. Go on painting. I'll be making you two some tea."

For a few minutes, as he warms the tea-pot, and brings the tea out of the cupboard, and drops in the recognised four teaspoonfulls, one for each of them, and one for the pot, the painter works desperately on. Presently the interrupter walks up to have another look at the picture. He stands at the painter's elbow, buttering the bosom of a loaf of bread, and cutting it off in thick rounds. "What are you going to put in, to bring the light up into that corner?" he asks, pointing with the butter-knife.

"I was thinking of a silver pot: what do you think yourself? Anyhow, Serafina, we've earned our tea." So work comes to an end for the day. That is the sole virtue of the interrupter—he keeps other people from over-working themselves, and Serafina at least is grateful.

All three will discuss the picture; how its lights and shadows are to be arranged into repose, and prevented from playing battledore and shuttlecock with the observer's eye; what colours are to be heightened, what toned down; what artifice of detail, what careful obscurity is to be introduced, and where; and so on, in a jargon incomprehensible to the lay mind, as the talk of any other trade. The discussion is not only between the artists; Serafina will bear her share, and likely enough make the most useful of the suggestions. For artist's models are not hampered, like the painters themselves, by knowing too much, and at the same time they are not ignorant as the ordinary picture buyer is ignorant. Some of them have been brought up in the studios from their earliest childhood, and all spend so much of their lives with the artists, and watch so many pictures from their inception to their failure or success, that they have a very practical knowledge of what makes a painting good or bad, and are often able to help a picture in other ways than by posing for it.

Indeed, most of them talk of the men for whom they pose as "my artists," and take a most personal interest in the fortunes of their pictures. A model is as happy as the painter when she can say "I was in the New Gallery this year, or the Academy, in so many different paintings." They are a class very much misunderstood. A girl who poses for an artist is not the immoral abandoned woman that the suburbs suppose her. She picks up something of an education, she learns something of art, she lives as interestingly, as usefully and as honestly as many of the people who condemn her. Many an artist owes his life to the Serafina, the Rosie, or the Brenda who, coming one morning to ask for a sitting, has found him ill and alone, with nobody to nurse him but an exasperated caretaker. Many a man has been kept out of the hospital, that dread of Bohemia, by the simple, kind-hearted model who has given up part of her working day to cooking his food for him, when he was too weak to do it himself, and then, tired after the long sittings, has brought her work with her,

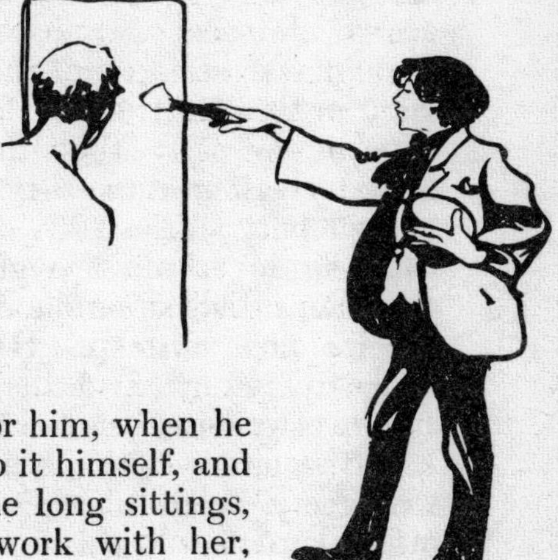

and sat down and sewed in his studio through the evening, and talked cheerful rubbish to him that has kept him from utter dis-heartenment.

There is rich material for novelists in the lives of these girls. One would have liked to be an actress, but had not a good enough voice. Another would have served behind a counter, if some artist had not noticed her, begged her to allow him to paint her, and then recommending her to his friends shown her this way to a livelihood. Some have stories that read like penny novelettes, and, tired of oppressive stepmothers, or guardians, or elder sisters, have deliberately left their homes, and, perhaps knowing a few artists, have taken up this work so that they might have their own lives to themselves. Some are even supporting their mothers and younger brothers or sisters. In nearly all cases they come to the studios through the accident of meeting a discerning artist in the street, and to some this accident happens so early that they are practically models all their lives. One child used to come to read fairy stories with me, and to cut out paper figures (a most joyous game), who had posed for artists since she was three years old, and was now fourteen. Her mother had been badly treated by her father, and the little girl and her two elder sisters had made enough to keep the family without his help. All three were very beautiful. Both the elder ones married artists, and the little girl told me when last I saw her that, so far as she was concerned, she was going to marry either an artist or a member of Parliament. Another model had been a gypsy, another was a genuine transplanted specimen of the rare species dairymaid as Izaak Walton knew it, another the runaway daughter of a shopkeeper in the North of France; the list could be made interminable.

As for the men models, they are not so numerous as the girls, and less interesting. They are nearly all Italians, tired of organ-grinding or ice-cream making, or else handsome old soldiers, or good-looking men who have come down in the world. Some of them are picturesque enough. One morning, still in bed, in lodgings over some studios, I heard a noise in my work-room, and jumping up, flung open the door, thinking to surprise my burglar in the act. In the middle of the room stood a charming old fellow, with a small knobbly head, very red skin, blue seafaring eyes, and a wispy white beard round cheeks and chin. He thought I was an artist, he said, and had come to see if he could be useful. We breakfasted, and he became talkative at once. He had been a sailor, had done well about the world, and had settled in California as a storekeeper, when he had been ruined by a big fire. "That was because I took Our Lord to mean insurance, when He said usury. It was set clear to me afterwards, but it was too late then, my stuff was gone." Since that time he had drifted, too old to pick up again, too proud to give in and enter the workhouse. He had worked his way to England on a ship he had once commanded, and an artist painting shipping had met him walking about the docks, and told him he could make a living as a model. "And I'm doing it," he said, "and it's not a bad life. There's hard times, and there's times rough on an old man, but I'm not so weak yet, thanks be, and I get tidily along. Yes. I'll have another pipe of that tobacco. It isn't often you gents have the right stuff."

But this has been a long digression from Serafina, the painter, and the interrupter, whom we left taking tea and discussing the picture. What do they do next? Perhaps if the daylight has not gone, and the interrupter has not been thoroughly efficient, a little more work may be done after tea. But it is more likely that the painter will wash his brushes, and go up to Soho to dine with the interrupter, possibly taking Serafina with him, if she has nothing to do with her evening. Or he may go to one of the artists' clubs.

In the old days there was no club in Chelsea, and the artists used to feed and talk at the Six Bells Tavern, the public-house in the King's Road, or else at one or other of the small inns along the riverside. I do not think the story of the founding of the Chelsea Art Club, in Church Street, has been printed before. It had been proposed that, as Chelsea had so long been associated with art, an exhibition should be held to illustrate the work of the principal painters who lived here. Meetings were held in the Six Bells, and a committee was appointed to report on the possibilities of the scheme. All the artists concerned met in one of the Manresa Road studios, with Mr. Stirling Lee, the sculptor, in the chair, to hear the result. Whistler and half a dozen other famous artists were there. The report was duly read, when some one got up and said that surely there was something that Chelsea needed more than an exhibition, and that was a club. "Club, club, club!" shouted everybody, and the exhibition was completely forgotten at once, and has never been held to this day. A Teutonic gentleman proposed that they should rent a room for the club in the Pier Hotel, which he pronounced, after the manner of Hans Breitmann, "Bier." Whistler rose, in his most dignified, most supercilious manner: "Gentlemen," he said, slowly, "Gentlemen, let us not start our club in any beer hotel—

let us start our club CLEAN." The result was the Chelsea Art Club, in a house of its own, the meeting place of all the Chelsea artists, and the centre of half the fun, the frivolity, the gossip of Chelsea studio life.

Another famous artists' club is the Langham Sketch Club, whose rooms are close behind the Queen's Hall. Artists meet there regularly, and draw and make pictures all in a room together, with a time limit set for the performance. At intervals they exhibit the harvest of their evenings on the walls. They have also merry parties, for men only, when the doors are opened by fantastical figures, and scratch entertainments go on all the time, and there are songs and jovial recitations. Nights there are as merry as any, and the rooms are full of celebrated men, and men about to be celebrated; for the club does not tolerate bunglers.

The painter might go to one of those places; or else, after a supper in Soho, or in one of the very few little restaurants in Chelsea, he might spend the evening in some one else's studio, perhaps in the same block of buildings as his own, for few of the studios are isolated, and there are often three, five, eight, or more under a single roof. The studio life is almost like the life of a university, with its friendliness, its sets, and their haughty attitude towards each other. There is the set that scorns the Academy and all its works; whose members never cross the threshold of Burlington House, and smile a little pityingly if you mention an R.A. with anything but contempt. For them the ideals and exhibitions of the new English movement, unless indeed they are bold Ishmaels and have for ever shaken the dust of exhibitions from their feet. Then there is the rather amusing set of people who laugh at the Academy, but recognise that it is the best picture shop in Europe, and exhibit there for their pocket's sake. And then there is the set made up largely of old Academy students, and of men with wives (who *will*, no matter what you say to them, care for material success), who regulate all their work by the Academy standards, beg advice from the R.A.'s, and live and die a hundred times in hope and despair between the sending in day and the day of last rejections from that most august, most oligarchic, most British of institutions.

The men of each set have a habit of

dropping in to talk away their evenings in particular studios. It is curious this: how one studio will be chosen without arrangement, by accident as it seems, and yet be made by custom so regular a rendezvous that its visitors would scarcely know what to do if they were asked to meet anywhere else. If you are at dinner in Soho with men of one set, then afterwards by some natural attraction you find the party setting out for Brown's place; if with men of another set, then assuredly before the night is out you will be smoking a cigarette at Robinson's. It is not that the man whose studio is so honoured is the cleverest, the leader of the set—he is often a mere camp-follower in whatever movement may be afoot. It is not even that he has the most comfortable rooms—one favourite studio is the poorest in a building, and so ill-furnished that if you visit it you are wise to bring your own chair. I do not know what the reason is. Some men are best in their kennels, others best out of them; and the atmosphere of some kennels is more companionable than that of others; there can be nothing else.

About nine o'clock the painter, if he has not gone to a club, will arrive, without particular effort, at one of these more hospitable studios. Perhaps there will be a piano in a corner, with a man playing over its keys in the dark. Another man will be looking at the prints in a book by the light of a candle. Perhaps there will be a witty little model telling stories and keeping everybody laughing. Perhaps there will be no more than a couple of friends, who no longer find talk necessary for intercourse, but can be perfectly contented in tobacco smoke and each other's silence.

They will greet him when he comes with a question about the new picture. He will tell them, of course, that it is going to be a failure, and they will tell him not to be a fool. And then they will sit on, smoking, playing chess, singing, talking of their plans for the year, or the idiosyncrasies of a refractory picture buyer, or the abominable vanity of some stout gentleman who wants to look slim in a portrait, and so on and so on. Late at night they will separate, and he will go home to have a last look at the picture, anxiously, sleepily, holding a flickering candle ; and then to sleep on the camp-bed in the corner of the studio, to dream of work and of the picture as he would like it to be, unaccountably more beautiful than he can make it, until he wakes next morning, hurries over the road to the cook-shop for his breakfast, and back again to be impatiently ready for the arrival of Serafina, late as usual, after the custom of her kind.

And so go twenty-four hours of an artist's life.

THE COUNTRY IN BOHEMIA

WILLIAM HAZLITT.

THE COUNTRY IN BOHEMIA

LONDON is full of people who keep the country in their hearts, and the life of studios, taverns, and newspaper offices is lived by many who would scorn the name of Londoner. One thinks himself a Devon man, another is a Scot, another, though he works in London all the year, calls the Lake Mountains home. It is so now; it has been so ever since the green fields drew away from London, and made town and country two hostile, different things. Hazlitt, talking metaphysically in the little tavern under Southampton Buildings, or seated in his favourite corner there, with a pot of ale before him for custom's sake, and a newspaper before his eyes, listening to the vain talk of "coffee-house politicians," must often have congratulated himself on having been able to ask from his heart for "the clear blue sky above my head, and the green turf beneath my feet, a winding road before me, and a three hours' march to dinner—and then to thinking." He can never have forgotten that he was more than the townsman, in that he had known the Great North Road.

Borrow was another of your countrymen in town. You remember—when he wished to fight his way among the hack writers with "Ancient Songs of Denmark, heroic and romantic, with notes philological, critical, and historical," or "The Songs of Ap Gwilym, the Welsh bard, also with notes critical, philological, and historical"—his disconcerting interview with the publisher:

"I am very sorry, sir," says Borrow, "to hear that you cannot assist me. I had hoped——"

"A losing trade, I assure you, sir; literature is a drug. Taggart (this to his clerk), what o'clock is it?"

"Well, sir, as you cannot assist me, I will now take my leave; I thank you sincerely for your kind reception, and will trouble you no longer."

"Oh don't go. I wish to have some further conversation with you, and perhaps I may hit on some plan to benefit you. I honour merit, and always make a point to encourage it when I can; but—Taggart, go to the bank, and tell them to dishonour the bill twelve months after date for thirty pounds which becomes due to-morrow. I am dissatisfied with that fellow who wrote the fairy tales, and intend to give him all the trouble in my power. Make haste. . . ."

I'll warrant Borrow was helped to keep his upper lip straight then, and afterwards, when he was dismally translating into German the publisher's own philosophical treatise, that proved the earth to be shaped like a pear and not "like an apple, as the fools of Oxford say," by the thought of country roads, and horses galloping, and his own stout legs that could walk with any in England, and his arms that could swing a hammer to a blacksmith's admiration.

And what of Bampfylde in an older time, who was not able, like Hazlitt and Borrow, to see the country again and again, but came here from it, to live miserably, and die with its vision in his heart? Southey, grave, hard-working, respectable as he was, felt something of the tragedy of that countryman's irregular life. Through the sedate and ordered phrases of this letter of his to Sir Samuel Egerton Brydges, the vivid, unhappy life of the man bursts through like blood in veins. The letter is long, but I quote it almost in full:—

KESWICK, *May* 10, 1809.

"SIR,

". . . It gives me great pleasure to hear that Bampfylde's remains are to be edited. The circumstances which I did not mention concerning him are these. They were related to me by Jackson, of Exeter, and minuted down immediately afterwards, when the impression which they made upon me was warm.

"He was the brother of Sir Charles, as you say. At the time when Jackson became intimate with him he was just in his prime, and had no other wish than to live in solitude, and amuse himself with poetry and music. He lodged in a farmhouse near Chudleigh, and would oftentimes come to Exeter in a winter morning, ungloved and open-breasted, before Jackson was up (though he was an early riser), with a pocket full of music or poems, to know how he liked them. His relations thought this was a sad life for a man of family, and forced him to London. The tears ran down Jackson's cheeks when he told me the story. 'Poor fellow,' he said, 'there did not live a purer creature, and, if they would have let him alone, he might have been alive now.'

"When he was in London, his feelings, having been forced out of their proper channel, took a wrong direction, and he soon began to suffer the punishment of debauchery. The Miss Palmer to whom he dedicated his Sonnets (afterwards, and perhaps still, Lady Inchiquin) was niece to Sir Joshua Reynolds. Whether Sir Joshua objected to his addresses on account of his irregularities in London, or on other grounds, I know not; but this was the commencement of his madness. He was refused admittance into the house; upon this, in a fit of half anger and half derangement, he broke the windows, and was (little to Sir Joshua's honour) sent to Newgate. Some weeks after this happened, Jackson went to London, and one of his first inquiries was for Bampfylde. Lady Bampfylde, his mother, said she knew little or nothing about him; that she had got him out of Newgate, and he was now in some beggarly place. 'Where?' 'In King Street, Holborn, she believed, but she did not know the number of the house.' Away went Jackson, and knocked at every door till he found the right. It was a truly miserable place; the woman of the house was one of the worst class of women in London. She knew that Bampfylde had no money, and that at that time he had been three days without food. When Jackson saw him there was all the levity of madness in his manner; his shirt was ragged and black as a coal-heaver's, and his beard of a two months' growth. Jackson sent out for food, and said he was come to breakfast with him; and he turned aside to a harpsichord in the room, literally, he said, to let him gorge himself without being noticed. He removed him from thence, and, after giving his mother a severe lecture, obtained for him a decent allowance, and left him, when he himself quitted town, in decent lodgings, earnestly begging him to write.

"But he never wrote; the next news was that he was in a private madhouse, and Jackson never saw him more. Almost the last time they met, he showed several poems, among others, a ballad on the murder of David Rizzio; such a ballad! said he. He came that day to dine with Jackson, and was asked for copies. 'I burned them,' was the reply; 'I wrote them to please you; you did not seem to like them, so I threw them in the fire.' After twenty years' confinement he recovered his senses, but not till he was dying of consumption. The apothecary urged him to leave Sloane Street (where he had always been as kindly treated as he could be) and go into his own country, saying that his friends in Devonshire would be very glad to see him. But he hid his face and answered, 'No, sir; they who knew me what I was, shall never see me what I am.' . . ."

His was a different case from that of Hazlitt leaving Wem, of De Quincey running from school, or of Goldsmith setting out from Lissoy. It is a sad story this of the strength of the town, of its coarse fingers on the throat of a wild bird, and I should like to pretend that there are no Bampfyldes in Bohemia to-day who have lost their poetry in London, and dare not go back to their own country, "lest those who knew them what they were, should see them what they are." It is a terrible thing to feel ashamed in the presence of the hills, and fearful that the spring has lost its power of refreshment.

But there are many stronger men, who have come to London because poetry or pictures will not support them in the villages they love, and carry a glad pride in their hearts that softens the blows, and eases the difficulties of the town. It is something as you walk disconsolate down a publisher's stairs, like a little boy from a whipping, to be able to pull up your despair with a stout breath, a toss of your head, a thought of the wind in your face, and the straight road over the moorland, with the peewits overhead; something, when eating a hard-boiled egg at a coffee-stall, to remember another occasion, when in greater straits you were less pusillanimous, and tossed away your last eighteenpence to feed and sleep royally in a little village inn, ready to face the world with empty purse and cheerful heart in the sunshine of the morning. Ay, it is a great thing to be a countryman, to know the smell of the hay when a cart rolls by to Covent Garden, and to dream in Paternoster Row of the broad open road, with the yellowhammer in the hedge and the blackthorn showing flower.

It is a very joyous thing for a countryman in town, when some small thing from the Happy Land breaks through the gloom or weariness or excitement of his irregular life, like a fountain in the dusk. For example, I have seldom been happier in Bohemia than when two old country songs that have, so far as I know, never been written down were sung to me in some dingy rooms over a set of studios by an artist's model I had never seen before.

There was a yellow fog outside and a lamp burned on my desk, in the ashamed manner of a lamp in daylight. It does not matter what article my brain was flogging itself to produce, for the article was never written.

My landlady had brought me up some beef and fried onions in a soup plate, but things were altogether too woeful for the enjoyment of lunch, when someone tapped at my door,

and almost instantly a dainty, slight girl, with a little brown felt hat on her head and a green cloak about her, opened the door and smiled at me from the threshold.

“ Do you need a model ? ” she asked.

I was so glad to see anything so young and fresh and beautiful in the dull lamplight of that fog-choked room, so heartened by the very sight of her, that I almost forgot to answer, and then, in an agony of fear lest she should go at once, when she saw that she was not in a studio, explained very awkwardly that I was very glad she had called, that it was an unpleasant day, that, that . . . . and could she stop to lunch.

She laughed, a clear country laugh, that made it possible for me to laugh too; and in a moment the gloom seemed to have vanished for the day, as she sat down as pretty as you please to share my beef and onions.

We came at once to talk of the country, and, afterwards, when we pulled our chairs up to the fire, and she let me light a cigarette for her, she was telling me of her old life, before she came to London, where she lived in a little village in Gloucestershire. Playing with the cigarette in her fingers, she told me how she used to get up to make her brother's breakfast before he went out to labour on the farm, how before that she had been at the village school, and how, when they had all been children, her old grandmother had used to sing to them every evening songs she had learnt in her youth. "Did she remember any of the songs?" I asked, hoping, and yet telling myself to expect no more than the modern jingles that have been made popular by print. "Why, yes, she remembered a few, but she could not sing as well as her old grandmother." And then, after a little entreaty, in that little dark dusty room in Bohemia, she came out with this ballad in a simple untrained voice that was very well suited to the words:

Oh it's of a fair damsel in Londin did dwell;
Oh for wit and for beauty her none could excel.
With her mistress and her master she servéd seven year,
And what followed after you quickely shall hear.

Oh I took my box upon my head. I gainéd along,
And the first one I met was a strong and able man.
He said, "My pretty fair maid, why are you going this way?
I'll show to you a nearer road across the counterey."

He took me by the hand, and he led me to the lane;
He said, "My pretty fair maid, I mean to tell you plain.
Deliver up your money without a fear or strife,
Or else this very moment I'll take away your life."

The tears from my eyes like fountains they did flow.
Oh where shall I wander? Oh where shall I go?
And so while this young feller was a feeling for his knife,
Oh this beautiful damsel, she took away his life.

I took my box upon my head. I gainéd along,
And the next one I met was a noble gentleman.
He said, "My pretty fair maid, where are you going so late?"
And what was that noise that I heard at yonder gate?

"I fear that box upon your head to yourself does not belong.
To your master or your mistress you have done something wrong;
To your mistress or your master you have done something ill,
For one moment from trimbeling you really can't stand still."

To my master or my mistress I have done nothing ill;
But I feel within my own dear heart it's a young man I do kill.
He dem'ded my money, but I soon let him know,
And now that able feller lies bleeding down below.

This gentleman got off his hoss to see what he had got;
He had three loaded pistols, some powder and some shot;
He had three loaded pistols, some powder and some ball,
And a knife and a whistle, more robbers for to call.

This gentleman blew the whistle, he blew it both loud and shrill,
And four more gallant robbers came trimbling down the hill.
Oh this gentleman shot one of them, and then most speedilee,
Oh this beautiful damsel, she shot the other three.

"And now, my pretty fair maid, for what you have done,
I'll make of you my charming bride before it is long.
I'll make of you my own dear bride, and that very soon,
For taking of your own dear path, and firing off a goon."

It was a strange thing to hear the gentle, lazy melody that carried those words in the foggy little London room. It was the stranger to hear the words and the air from a girl like this one, who had now taken off her hat, and lay back in the ricketty deck-chair, smoothing her tangled golden head, and ready for another cigarette. The setting was London of London: the song and its melody carried the very breath of the country into the room; the girl, an artist's model, smoking cigarettes, ready I have no doubt to compare with knowledge the merits of cherry brandy and benedictine, and yet as happy in singing that old tune as her grandmother had been long ago in the far away Gloucestershire cottage. "Did she know any more?" I asked, and she sang me several that I knew already, and then, blushing, said there was another song she knew with a prettier tune even than the first; but she was ashamed of the words. She would hum the melody.

I wanted the words. "But your grandmother used to sing them," I protested.

"Yes," she said, "but when granny sang them, she used to close her mouth so, and then she would look at us, and blush, and then she would look into the fire all the while she sang."

I pointed to the fire, and she looked into it, and laughed, and then, with the blood coming and going very prettily in her face, she sang to a most delicate, happy melody, this wicked song:

> "Good morning to you, my fair pretty maid."
> "Oh, twice good morning, sir," she said.
> "What! Are you milking all alone?"
> "I am," replied sweet fair lovely Joan.
>
> Then he pulled out a purse of gold,
> As much as her two hands could hold.
> "All this I will give for your maidenhead;
> Your cheeks they shine like the roses red."
>
> "Oh give me the gold all in my hand,
> That I may neither stay nor stand,
> For it will be more value to me
> Than twenty maidenheads," cried she.
>
> As he looked round for bed that night,
> She mounted on his steed milk-white;
> He hoop'd, he coop'd, but 'twas all in vain;
> She never dared once look back again.

She rode till she came to her true love's gate.
"Oh, pray don't keep or make me wait,
For I've robbed him of his steed and gold,
And given him the empty purse to hold."

She pleased her true love to the heart,
To think how well she had played her part.
"Oh, to-morrow morning we'll get wed;
My love shall enjoy my maidenhead."

Soon after that she stood up, laughing because there was no mirror, to put on her little hat. I begged her to stay and come to dinner with me in Soho, but she had a business engagement, to pose for a pen and ink illustrator in the evening. She left me, and it was as if the blue sky had shown for a moment through the clouds and disappeared. The afternoon was foggy London once again, and Gloucestershire seemed distant as the Pole.

* * * * *

In talking of countrymen and their comforts in town, I cannot think how I forgot to mention the consolation of a village reputation far away. When editors refuse your works, and Academies decline to hang your pictures, you have always the reflection of the lady of the nursery rhyme:

"There was a young lady of Beverley
Whose friends said she sang very cleverly;
'She'll win great renown
In great London town,'
So said the good people of Beverley.

"But in London this lady of Beverley
Found all her best notes fell but heavily ;
And when this she did find,
She said, 'Never mind,
They still think me a songbird at Beverley.'"

It is a reflection often made by countrymen in town.

OLD AND NEW SOHO

OLD AND NEW SOHO

SOHO has always been a merry place. Even at the time when Keats wrote scornfully of it in a letter to Haydon:

> " For who would go
> Into dark Soho,
> To chatter with dank-haired critics,
> When he might stay
> In the new-mown hay
> And startle the dappled prickets ? "

—even then there were plenty of fellows, more merry than critical, who sported as playfully in its narrow streets as ever poets did in hayfields. A street out of Soho Square, now so heavily odorous of preserved fruit, from the factory at the corner, was for a time the home of so redoubtable a merrymaker, so sturdy a Bohemian, as Pierce Egan, the author of "Life in London, or the Day and Night Scenes of Jerry Hawthorn, Esq., and his elegant friend Corinthian Tom, accompanied by Bob Logic the Oxonian, in their Rambles and Sprees through the Metropolis." A jolly book indeed, whose very pictures—— but

Thackeray has described them in a manner inimitable by any clumsy careful fellow:—

"First there is Jerry arriving from the country, in a green coat and leather gaiters, and being measured for a fashionable suit at Corinthian House, by Corinthian Tom's tailor. Then away for the career of pleasure and fashion. The Park! delicious excitement! The theatre! the saloon!! the greenroom!!! Rapturous bliss—the opera itself! and then perhaps to Temple Bar, *to knock down a Charley there!* There are Jerry and Tom, with their tights and little cocked hats, coming from the opera—very much as gentlemen in waiting on Royalty are habited now. There they are at Almack's itself, amidst a crowd of highbred personages, with the Duke of Clarence himself looking at their dancing. Now, strange change, they are in Tom Cribbs' parlour, where they don't seem to be a whit less at home than in fashion's gilded halls: and now they are at Newgate, seeing the irons knocked off the malefactors' legs previous to execution. . . . Now we haste away to merrier scenes: to Tattersall's (ah, gracious powers! what a funny fellow that actor was who performed Dicky Green in that scene at the play!); and now we are at a private party, at which Corinthian Tom is waltzing (and very gracefully, too, as you must confess) with Corinthian Kate, whilst Bob Logic, the Oxonian, is playing on the piano!"

I can never see this giddy rampant book

without thinking of a paragraph in it, that shows us, through the Venetian-coloured glass of Mr. Egan's slang:—

"Mr. Hazlitt, in the evening, lolling at his ease upon one of Ben Medley's elegant couches, enjoying the reviving comforts of a good *tinney* (which is a fire), smacking his *chaffer* (which is his tongue) over a glass of old hock, and topping his *glim* (which is a candle) to a *classic* nicety, in order to throw a *new light* upon the elegant leaves of Roscoe's 'Life of Lorenzo de Medici,' as a composition for a New Lecture at the Surrey Institution. This is also Life in London."

I like to think of Hazlitt at Ben Medley's, who was "a well-known hero in the Sporting World, from his determined contest with the late pugilistic phenomenon, Dutch Sam." It is pleasant, is it not? Almost as delightful as that glimpse of him driving back from the great fight between Hickman and Neate, when "my friend set me up in a genteel drab great coat and green silk handkerchief (which I must say became me exceedingly)."

Pierce Egan knew well the Bohemian life of his day. There is a story that is a better compliment to his spirit than his head. Some of his friends lifted him, dead drunk after a masquerade, into a cab, put some money in his pocket, gave the cabby his address, and announced that he was a foreign nobleman. Off drives cabby, and finds the house, with ten bell-pulls, ringing to the rooms belonging to the different tenants. Cheerfully, as one with nobility in his cab, he tugs the whole ten. From every window indignant night-capped heads deny relationship with any foreign nobleman. "But I've brought him from the masquerade, and he's got money in his pocket." Instantly everybody in the house runs downstairs and out into the street. Egan's wife recognised her errant husband, and, with the help of the other lodgers, carried him to his room. He was out on the spree again the following day.

Egan was a gay fellow, wrote voluminously, lived vigorously, and if he did not deserve it in any other way, fully earned the title of a Man of Letters by a passage in the dedication of his most famous book to his Majesty George IV. :—

"Indeed the whole chapter of 'Life in London' has been so repeatedly perused by your Majesty, in such a variety of shapes, from the *elegant* A, the *refined* B, the *polite* C, the *lively* D, the *eloquent* E, the *honest* F, the *stately* G, the *peep o' day* H, the *tasteful* I, the *manly* J, the *good* K, the *noble* L, the *stylish* M, the *brave* N, the *liberal* O, the *proud* P, the *longheaded* Q, the *animated* R, the *witty* S, the *flash* T, the *knowing* U, the *honourable* V, the *consummate* W, the *funny* X, the *musical* Y, and the *poetical* Z, that it would only be a waste of your Majesty's valuable time to expatiate further upon this subject."

But Soho has known more lettered men

than Egan. De Quincey, young and new to London, before he had lost the poor woman of the streets who, out of her own penury, bought port wine for him when he was likely to die on a doorstep in Soho Square, found lodging in an unfurnished house in Greek Street. The ground floor of the house was occupied by a rascally lawyer, whose best quality was a devotion to literature that led him to shelter the boy scholar, or at least to allow him to sleep on the floor of nights, with waste papers for a pillow, and an old horse-blanket for a covering, that he shared with a hunger-bitten child.

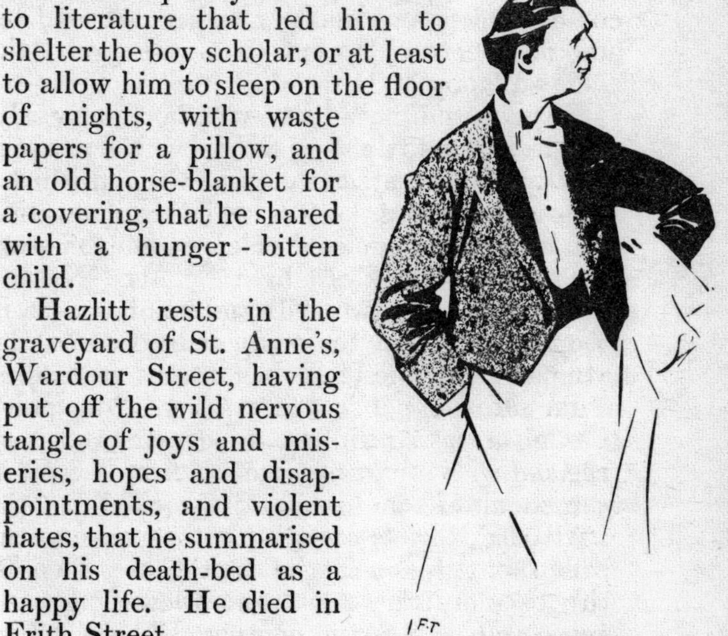

Hazlitt rests in the graveyard of St. Anne's, Wardour Street, having put off the wild nervous tangle of joys and miseries, hopes and disappointments, and violent hates, that he summarised on his death-bed as a happy life. He died in Frith Street.

In Gerrard Street, Dryden lived at No. 43, and doubtless found it very convenient for walking down of an afternoon to the coffee-houses about Covent Garden. Burke lived for a time at No. 37, and the greatest of all clubs, The Club, of Johnson, Goldsmith and Reynolds, met at the Turk's Head Tavern in the same street.

There were clubs here in the early nineteenth century, and Thackeray described one of them in "The Newcomes": "We tap at a door in an old street in Soho: an old maid with a kind comical face opens the door, and nods friendly, and says, 'How do, sir? ain't seen you this ever so long. How do, Mr. Noocom?' 'Who's here?' 'Most everybody's here.' We pass by a little snug bar, in which a trim elderly lady is seated by a great fire, on which boils an enormous kettle; while two gentlemen are attacking a cold saddle of mutton and West Indian pickles: hard by Mrs. Nokes the landlady's elbow—with mutual bows—we recognise Hickson the sculptor, and Morgan, intrepid Irish chieftain, chief of the reporters of the *Morning Press* newspaper. We pass through a passage into a back room, and are received with a roar of welcome from a crowd of men, almost invisible in the smoke."

All the districts of London that have once made themselves a special atmosphere, keep it with extraordinary tenacity. Fleet Street is one example, Soho is another. The Turk's Head has disappeared, Thackeray's club is not to be found; but every Tuesday a dozen, more or less, of the writers of the day meet at a little restaurant in the very street where Goldsmith and Johnson walked to meet their friends. This is the Mont Blanc, a very old house, whose walls have once been panelled. In the rooms upstairs, the mouldings of the panels can be felt plainly through the canvas that has been stretched across them and papered to save the cost of painting. And all over Soho are similar small meeting places, where irregulars of all sorts flock to lunch and dine. Still, in some of the upper rooms of the streets where De Quincey walked to warm himself before sleeping on the floor, the student life goes on. Still in some of the upper windows may be seen the glitter of a candle-light where a scholar, probably foreign, pores over a book in the hours when the British Museum is closed to him. And in a hundred of the small rooms in the piles of Soho flats, small rooms furnished with a bed, a chair, and a table that also serves for a washing-stand, are there young actors and actresses, studying great parts and playing small ones, eager to be Macduff and content meanwhile to represent the third witch on the boards of a suburban theatre, copying the mannerisms of Miss Edna May, and keeping alive by smiling at the pit from the medley of the ballet.

* * * * *

It is odd to think of the days when a shilling dinner was beyond achievement, when a sandwich and a couple of bananas seemed a supper for a Shakespeare. Yet those were happy days, and had their luxuries. There are sandwiches and sandwiches. In one of the narrower streets that run up from Shaftesbury Avenue towards Oxford Street, there is a shop whose proprietor is an enthusiast, a facile virtuoso in their manufacture. He is an amateur in the best sense, and no selfish arrogant fellow who will allow none but himself to be men of taste. You stand in the middle of his shop, with all kinds of meats arranged on the shelves about you, a knife on every dish. Veal, potted liver, chicken artfully prepared, *paté de foie gras* or a substitute, tongue spiced and garnished, tongue potted and pressed, lobster paste, shrimp paste, cockle paste, and half a hundred other luscious delicacies, wait in a great circle about you, like paints on a palette ; while you stand hesitating in the middle, and *compose* your sandwich, a touch of this, a taste of that, a suspicion of this, a sprinkling of that again, while he, at once a skilful craftsman and a great genius, does the rough handiwork, and executes your design, often, like the great man of the art school, contributing some little detail of his own that is needed for perfection, and presents you finally with the complete work of art, cut in four for convenient eating, for sixpence only, an epicurean triumph, and enough of it to sustain you till the morning.

After your sandwich, you will find, in Little Pulteney Street, if I am not mistaken in the name, a man with bananas on a hand barrow, and likely enough an Italian woman with a red or green shawl about her head, turning the handle of a barrel-organ. With these things it is easy to be happy. How happy I used to be, walking along that street peeling and eating my bananas, while my heart throbbed bravely to the music of the organ. Sometimes a couple of children would be dancing in the street, as nautch girls might enliven the supper of an Indian potentate; and often some one would be singing the words to the barrel-organ's melodies. What were the favourite tunes? Ah yes:

> "Dysy, Dysy, give me yer awnser, do;
> I'm arf cryzy all fur the love of you,"

and

> "As you walk along
> The Bar de Bullong
> With a independent air,
> You 'ear the girls declare
> There goes the millyonaire,
> The man wot broke the benk at Monte *Car*lo."

Yes; those were very happy days, and you, O reader, lose much if the fulness of your purse, or the delicacy of your ear, deprives you of such an enjoyment.

When your income rises beyond the contentment of bananas and sandwich for dinner, or earlier, when the sale of a picture, or a longer article than usual, entitles you to a tremulous extravagance, you have an adventurous choice to make among the Soho restaurants. Every evening after half-past six or seven, Soho takes on itself a new atmosphere. It is grubby and full of romantic memory by day. At night it is suddenly a successful place, where the proprietors of little restaurants are able to retire upon the fortunes they have made there. The streets, always crowded with foreigners, now suffer odder costumes than in daylight. Artists, poets, writers, actors, music-hall performers, crowd to the special restaurants that custom reserves for their use. I do not know how many small eating-houses there are in Soho ; though I set out once, in a flush of recklessness at the sale of a book, to eat my way through the lot of them ; the plan was, to dine at a different restaurant every night, taking street by street, until I had exhausted them all, and could retire with unrivalled experience. The scheme fell through, partly because I fell in love with one or two places, so that my feet insisted on carrying me through their doors, when my conscience announced that duty to the programme demanded a supper elsewhere, and partly because of a relapse into impecuniosity that compelled a return to the diet of bananas and sandwiches.

Alas that this should be a record of fact. What mansions of the stomach could I not describe, what sumptuous palaces, where wine and Munich lager flow from taps on every table, where food is as good in the mouth as in prospect, where landlords and proprietors stand upon their dignity, and refuse money as an insult to their calling. How perfectly could I reconstruct Soho in a gastronomic dream. Unfortunately I am bound as tight to fact as to penury.

The first Soho restaurant I knew was Roche's, now Béguinot's, in Old Compton Street. A lean painter took me; it was a foggy night, and we crossed Cambridge Circus with difficulty, and then, almost groping our way along the pavement, found the door, and stepped into the glamour and noise of the long room that you enter from the street. The painter wished to show me the whole place. We went right through to the inner room where we so often dined in later years, and downstairs to the hot little inferno, where a few brave spirits descend to feed and talk. The painter nodded to men in both rooms, and then turned to me. "This is Bohemia," he said; "what do you think of it?" We went back into the front room, and sat down behind the long table, so that I could see the whole place, and observe the people who came in.

Opposite our long table were half a dozen small ones placed along the wall, and at one of these sat a very splendid old man. His long white hair fell down over the collar of his velvet coat, and now and again he flung back his head, so that his hair all rippled in the light, and then he would bang his hand carefully upon the table, so as not to hurt it, and yet to be impressive, as he declaimed continually to a bored girl who sat opposite him, dressed in an odd mixture of fashion and Bohemianism. They seemed a queer couple to be together, until the painter told me that the man was one of the old set, who had come to the place for years, and remembered the old mad days when every one dressed in a luxuriously unconventional manner, like so many Theophile Gautiers. The painter, who was a realist, referred scornfully to the old fellow as "a piece of jetsam left by the romantic movement." There have been such a number of romantic movements in the last thirty years that it was impossible to know what he meant. But the tradition is still current at the Soho dinner tables that there were a few grand years in which we rivalled the Quartier in costume, and outdid Montmartre in extravagant conversation. It was pathetic to think of the old Romantic as a relic of that glorious time, alone in his old age, still living the life of his youth.

All down our long table there were not two faces that did not seem to me then to bear the imprint of some peculiar genius. Some were assuredly painters, others journalists, some very obviously poets, and there were several, too, of those amateur irregulars, who are always either exasperating or charming. The painter pointed out man after man by name. There was So-and-So, the musical critic; there was somebody else, who painted like Watteau: "ridiculous ass," commented my realistic friend; there was So-and-So, the editor of an art magazine; there a fellow who had given up art for a place in his father's business, but yet kept up his old acquaintanceships with the men more faithful to their ideals.

These Soho dinners are excellently cooked and very cheap. Only the wine is dearer in England than in France. There, you can get a carafon for a few pence, and good it is. But here the cheapest half-bottle is tenpence, and often disappointing. The wise drink beer. It is Charles Godfrey Leland who, in his jovial scrap of autobiography, ascribes all the vigour and jolly energy of his life to the strengthening effects of Brobdingnagian draughts of lager beer, drunk under the tuition of the German student. It is good companionable stuff, and a tankard of it costs only sixpence, or less.

In the same street with Béguinot's, a little nearer Piccadilly Circus, there is the Dieppe, a cheaper place, but very amusing. We used to feed there not for the sake of the food so much as for the pictures. Round the walls are several enormous paintings, some of which suggest Botticelli's Primavera in the most ridiculous manner, only that all the figures are decently clothed in Early Victorian costume. It is a real joy to dine there, and observe them. They are the dearest funny pictures that I know.

On the other side of the street is a white-fronted restaurant kept by a Monsieur Brice, to whom, through several years, I have been faithful. Night after night I have walked through the glitter and the dusk of the Soho streets, past the little tobacco shop where they sell real Caporal tobacco, one whiff of which transports you as if in an enchanted cloud to the Boul' Mich', where the chansonniers sing their own ballads, to the Bal Bullier and the students' balls, and make you a Parisian in a moment. I have walked along there night after night, and turned in at the small side door, and through into the little white back room, where the best of waiters kept a corner table. What suppers have vanished in that inner room, how many bottles of dark Munich beer have flowed to their appointed havens. Here the Benns, that little painter and his wife, used to join us, and sit and talk and smoke, planning new pictures that were to be better than all that had been done before, talking over stories as yet unwritten, and enjoying great fame in obscurity. Here too used other friends to come, so that we often sat down a merry half-dozen at the table, and enjoyed ourselves hugely and also other people. That is one of the chief merits of Soho dinners —the company is always entertaining. Sometimes there would be an old philosopher at the table opposite, who would solemnly drink his half-bottle, and then smoke a cigarette over some modern book. One day he leaned across towards our table with Haeckel's "Riddle of the Universe" in his hand. "Read this book, young people," he said, "but you should read it as you read *Punch*." That was his introduction to our party, and thenceforward, when he had finished his meal, he would always smoke his cigarette with us, and, smoothing his white beard with a pensive hand, employ himself upon our instruction in philosophy.

On other evenings, strangers would come in, and we would guess their ideals from their manners of unfolding their napkins—the gay flourish meant the artist, the deliberate disentanglement the man of prose, the careless fling the poet, and so on—or perhaps one of our enigmas would join in our talk, and puzzle us the more. So many of the faces were far from ordinary, so many had the inexpressible something in their lines that suggests an interesting mind. We were content to let them remain enigmas, and construed them each one of us to please himself.

Once there was a wedding party at a longer table, made by joining the three small ones at one side of the room. The bride was a pretty model, the man a tousled artist; probably, we agreed, a very inferior craftsman, but certainly an excellent fellow, since he insisted on our joining his company, which was made up of others like himself, with their attendant ladies. He and his bride were off to Dieppe for an inexpensive honeymoon, so that the feast could not be prolonged. At half-past eight the supper was done, and in a procession of hansom cabs we drove to Victoria, and cheered them off by the evening boat train, the two of them leaning out of the window, and tearfully shouting of their devotion to art, to each other, and to us, an excited heterogeneous crowd, who sang "Auld Lang Syne," "God Save the King," "The Marseillaise," and the *Faust* "Soldiers' Chorus," according to nationality, in an inextricable tangle of discord. That was a great night.

The Boulogne, the Mont Blanc, Pinoli's, the France, and many another little restaurant knew us in those days; there was scarcely one, from Brice's and the Gourmet's in the south, to the Venice, at the Oxford Street end of Soho Street, that had not suffered our merry dinner parties. There was not one that was not in some way or other linked with a memory of delight. The waiters, Auguste, Alphonse, Jean, le gros Paul, le grand Renard, all were our friends, and joked with us over our evil dialect and our innumerable acquaintance. It was le grand Renard, that great man, who elaborated the jest of greeting us every time, as soon as we entered, with "Ah, bon soir, Messieurs. Your friend M'sieur So and So has not been here to-day, nor M'sieur So and So, nor M'sieur So and So, nor M'sieur So and So, nor M'sieur So and So, nor M'sieur So and So," as far as his breath would carry him in an incoherent string of fantastic names, real and invented, that delighted us every time.

COFFEE-HOUSES ABOUT SOHO

COFFEE-HOUSES ABOUT SOHO

THE day that Casanova, travelling as the Chevalier de Seingalt, arrived in London, he strolled some little way from his lodging through the old streets of Soho, then as now the Italian quarter. Presently, he says, "I saw a lot of people in a coffee-house, and I went in. It was the most ill-famed coffee-house in London, and the meeting place of the scum of the Italian population. I had been told of it at Lyons, and had made up my mind never to go there; but chance often makes us turn to the left when we want to go to the right. I ordered some lemonade, and was drinking it, when a stranger who was seated near me took a news-sheet from his pocket, printed in Italian. He began to make corrections in pencil on the margin, which led me to suppose he was an author. I watched him out of curiosity, and noticed that he scratched out the word *ancora*, and wrote it at the side, *anchora*. This barbarism irritated me. I told him that for four centuries it had been written without an *h*."

"I agree with you," he answered, "but I am quoting Boccaccio, and in quotations one must be exact."

"I humbly beg your pardon; I see you are a man of letters."

"A very modest one; my name is Martinelli."

"I know you by reputation; you are a cousin of Casabigi's, who has spoken of you; I have read some of your satires."

"May I ask to whom I have the honour of speaking?"

"My name is Seingalt. Have you finished your edition of the 'Decameron'?"

"I am still working at it, and trying to get more subscribers."

"Will you allow me to be of the number?"

He put me down for four copies, at a guinea a copy, and was surprised to hear I had only been in London an hour.

"Let me see you home," he said; "you will lose your way else."

When we were outside he told me I had been in the Orange Coffee-House, the most disreputable in all London.

"But you go."

"I go because I know the company, and am on my guard against it."

"Do you know many people here?"

"Yes, but I only pay court to Lord Spencer. I work at literature, am all alone, earn enough for my wants. I live in furnished lodgings, I own twelve shirts and the clothes I stand up in, and I am perfectly contented."

That dialogue might serve well enough for an exaggerated description of our own day. For the people of this book are willing to drink anywhere but in the more tame and expensive places of the West End. They "know the company and are on their guard against it," and go cheerfully where they may get most amusement at the smallest cost.

The coffee-houses best loved by the Bohemians are not so disreputable as the Orange; I doubt if their reputations can have gone far beyond Soho. But they have atmospheres of their own; and they are not places where you are likely to meet any one oppressively more respectable or better dressed than yourself. I am thinking of two small houses in particular —"The Moorish Café" and "The Algerian." Beside these there are many others, and a few neater, more luxurious, more expensive, that help to wean the Bohemian from Bohemia; and then there are the big drinking palaces by Leicester Square and Piccadilly Circus, where he goes when he needs the inspiration of a string band, or the interest of a crowd of men and women.

Near the Oxford Street end of Soho Street, on the left-hand side as you walk towards Soho Square, is a small green painted shop, with a window full of coffee cups, and pots, and strainers of a dozen different designs. Looking through the window, that is dimmed likely enough with steam, you may see a girl busied with a big coffee-grinding machine, and watch the hesitant blue flames of the stove on which the coffee is stewed. Opening the door, you step into a babble of voices, and find yourself in a tiny Moorish Café. The room is twisted and narrow, so that you must have a care, as you walk, for other people's coffee cups upon the small round tables. At every table men will be sitting, blowing through their half-closed lips long jets of scented smoke that disturb continually the smoke-filled atmosphere. Some will be playing at cards, some at backgammon, some talking eagerly among themselves. Dark hair, dark eyes, sallow-skinned faces everywhere, here and there a low caste Englishman, and sometimes, if you are lucky, a Bohemian in emerald corduroy, lolling broadly on his chair and puffing at a porcelain pipe. Sit down near him, and it is ten to one that you will be engaged in a wordy battle of acting, of poetry, or of pictures, before the sediment has had time to settle in your coffee.

The coffee is thick and dark and sweet; to drink it alone, and to smoke with it an Eastern cigarette, is to hear strange Moorish melodies, to dream of white buildings with green-painted porticoes, to see the card-players as gambling dragomans, to snatch at a coloured memory from the Arabian Nights. The material for the dream is all about you; gaudy pictures in bright blues and oranges hang on the walls; there is Stamboul in deliciously impossible perspective, there the tomb of the Prophet, there an Ottoman warship, there Noah's Ark, with a peacock on the topmast, a serpent peering anxiously from a porthole, and Noah and his family flaunting it in caftans and turbans on the poop; from the brackets of the flickering incandescent lamps are hung old Moorish instruments, tarboukas, and gambas, dusty, with slackened strings, and yet sufficient, in the dream, to send the tunes of the desert cities filtering through the thick air of the room.

"The Algerian" is in Dean Street, close by the Royalty Theatre, where Coquelin played *Cyrano de Bergerac* and kept a whole party, French painters and English writers, quavering between laughter and tears, uplifted with pride that there could be such men as Cyrano, and joy that there was yet such an actor as Coquelin. It is on the same side of the street, a plain square window, thoroughly orthodox, with "The Algerian Restaurant" written over the top.

Behind a small counter sits Madame, knitting, smiling to all her acquaintance that come in, and selling neat brown packages of wonderful coffee. Beyond is an inner room, whose walls are covered with cocoanut matting, and decorated with tiny mirrors, and advertisements of special drinks. If you can get a corner seat in that crowded little room, you may be happy for an evening, with a succession of coffees and a dozen cigarettes. Sometimes there will be a few women watching the fun, but more often there will be none but men, mostly French or Italian, who play strange card games and laugh and curse at each other. There used to be a charming notice on the wall, which I cannot remember accurately.

> ANYONE CAUGHT GAMBLING OR
> PLAYING FOR MONEY
> Will be kicked into the gutter
> and not picked up again.
> PROPRIETOR.

It ran something like that, but it has now been replaced by a less suggestive placard.

Also there used to be another room downstairs, a gay companionable place, where I have played a penny whistle and seen some dancing to my music. Here we used to come after supper, to drink coffee, smoke cigarettes, and argue according to custom. Here would young Frenchmen bring their ladies, and talk freely in their own tongue. Here would we too bring our young women. It used to amuse me to notice the sudden hush that fell on the talk of all the couples and argumentative people, when the grim Police Inspector and his important bodyguard stumped heavily down the stairs, stood solemnly for a moment in the middle of the room, and then went slowly up the stairs again ——and the flood of excited chatter in several languages that followed their disappearance.

It is impossible to leave the Algerian without

remembering the wonderful big dog who used to be a visitor in the room below. He was a very large ruddy collie. Left to himself he was an easy-going fellow who would accept the hospitality of anybody who had anything to spare; but his master had only to say one word, and he would not dip his nose in the daintiest prettiest dish of coffee in the world. He was a gentleman of nice manners; if his master directed his attention to any lady who happened to be there, and whisper in his silky ear, "Toujours la politesse," immediately, with the gravity of an Ambassador, he would walk across and lift a ceremonial paw. It is sad that the room is now filled with lumber that was once so gay with humanity. But perhaps it will be opened again.

Close round the corner opposite the Algerian is a pretty white café, with a big window of a thousand little leaded panes, through which it is impossible to see. The whole suggestion of the outside is comfort and secluded luxury. And indeed so it is; you go there when you are a success; or, not being one of the famous or opulent, when, having just sold a book or a picture, you feel as if you were. Its air is very different from the friendly untidiness of the other two places. White cloths are on the tables, a little cut-glass is scattered about, and there are red and white flowers in silver vases—it is all so neat that I would not describe it, if it were not a favourite place of the more fortunate of the Bohemians, and if it had not been so sweet a suggestion of what might sometime be.

I came here in the pride of my first twenty-guinea cheque, and was introduced with due ceremony to Jeanne downstairs, pretty little Jeanne, who says most mournfully that some one has told her from the lines of her hand that she will not be married till she is two-and-thirty—eleven whole years to wait. My companion was a literary agent, who showed me three successes, two novelists and a critic, out of the half-dozen people who were sitting at the other tables. I almost wished he had not brought me, until Jeanne came back with black coffee in tall straight glasses, and some excellent cigarettes, when I changed my mind, and thought how often I would come here, if the world should turn good critic, and recognise in solid wealth the merit of my masterpieces.

Across Shaftesbury Avenue, past the stage doors of Daly's and the Hippodrome, through the narrow asphalt passage that is often crowded with ballet girls and supers, walking up and down before the times of their performances at one or other theatre, you find your way into the brilliance of Leicester Square. The Alhambra and the Empire fill two sides of it with light, and Shakespeare stands on a pedestal between them, resting his chin on his hand in melancholy amazement.

Downstairs at the corner of the Square there

is the drinking-hall of the Provence, a long L-shaped room, with a band playing in a corner, and smaller rooms opening out of the first, and seeming a very multitude of little caverns from the repetition of the mirrors with which they are lined. There are frescoes on the walls of the larger room, of gnomes swilling beer, and tumbling head first into vats, and waving defiance at the world with all the bravado of a mug of ale. Fat pot-bellied little brutes they are, and so cheerfully conceived that you would almost swear their artist had been a merry fellow, and kept a tankard on the steps of his ladder where he sat to paint them.

There is always a strange crowd at this place, dancers and singers from the music halls, sad women pretending to be merry, coarse women pretending to be refined, and men of all types grimacing and clinking glasses with the women. And then there are the small groups indifferent to everything but the jollity and swing of the place, thumping their beer mugs on the table over some mighty point of philosophy or criticism, and ready to crack each others' heads for joy in the arguments of Socialism or Universal Peace.

I was seated at a table here one night, admiring the picture in which a gnome pours some hot liquid on another gnome who lies shrieking in a vat, when I noticed a party of four men sitting at a table opposite. Three were obviously hangers-on of one or other of the arts, the sort of men who are proud of knowing an actor or two to speak to, and are ready to talk with importance of their editorial duties on the *Draper's Compendium* or the *Toyshop Times.* The fourth was different. A huge felt hat banged freely down over a wealth of thick black hair, bright blue eyes, an enormous black beard, a magnificent manner (now and again he would rise and bow profoundly, with his hat upon his heart, to some girls on the other side of the room), a way of throwing his head back when he drank, of thrusting it forward when he spoke, an air of complete abandon to the moment and the moment's thought; he took me tremendously. He seemed to be delighting his friends with impromptu poetry. I did a mean but justifiable thing, and carried my pot of beer to a table just beside him, where I could see him better, and also hear his conversation. It was twaddle, but such downright, spirited, splendid twaddle, flung out from the heart of him in a grand, careless way that made me think of largesse royally scattered on a mob. His blue twinkling eyes decided me. When, a minute or two later, he went out, I followed, and found him vociferating to his gang upon the pavement. I pushed in, so as to exclude them, and asked him:

"Are you prose or verse?"

"I write verse, but I dabble in the other thing." It was the answer I had expected.

"Very good. Will you come to my place

to-morrow night at eight? Tobacco. Beer. Talk."

"I love beer. I adore tobacco. Talking is my life. I will come."

"Here is my card. Eight o'clock to-morrow. Good-night." And so I left him.

He came, and it turned out that he worked in a bank from ten to four every day, and played the wild Bohemian every night. His beard was a disguise. He spent his evenings seeking for adventure, he said, and apologised to me for earning an honest living. He was really delightful. So are our friendships made; there is no difficulty about them, no diffidence; you try a man as you would a brand of tobacco; if you agree, then you are friends; if not, why then you are but two blind cockchafers who have collided with each other in a summer night, and boom away again each in his own direction.

Over the road there is the Café de l'Europe, where, also downstairs, there is an even larger drinking hall. Huge bizarre pillars support a decorated ceiling, and beneath them there are a hundred tables, with variegated maroon-coloured cloths, stained with the drippings of tankards and wine-glasses. There is a band here too, in a balcony halfway up the stairs. This place, like all the other cafés, is not exclusively Bohemian; we are only there on sufferance, in isolated parties, and it is a curious contrast to look away to the clerks, demi-mondaines, and men about town, sitting at the other tables; faces that have left their illusions with their youth, faces with protruding lips and receding chins, weak, foolish faces with watery eyes, office boys trying to be men, and worn-out men trying to be boys, and women ridiculously dressed and painted. We used to go there most when we were new to journalism, and we found it a great place for planning new periodicals. Eight or nine of us used to meet there, and map out a paper that was to startle the town, and incidentally give us all the opportunities that the present race of misguided editors denied. We would select our politics, choose our leader-writers, and decide to save quarrels by sharing the dramatic criticism between us all. We would fight lustily over the title, and have a wrangle over the form. Some would wish to ape the *Saturday Review*, some would desire a smaller, more convenient shape for putting in the pocket, and others, commercially minded, would suggest a gigantic size that might make a good show on the bookstalls. We would stand lagers again and again, proud in the knowledge of our new appointments, leader-writers, editors, dramatic critics everyone of us. And then, at last, after a whole evening of beer and extravagance, and happy pencilled calculations of our immediate incomes, based on a supposed sale of 100,000 copies weekly (we were sure of that at least), we would come suddenly to fact. The Scotch poet, whom we usually elected business manager on these occasions, would smile grimly, and say, " Now, gentlemen, the matter of finance. There will be printers and papermakers to pay. Personally, and speaking for myself alone, I will give all that I possess."

" And how much is that?" we would cry, although we guessed.

" Well "—and he would make great show of rumaging his pockets—" it seems that I was cleaned right out of bullion by that last lot of beer. O'Rourke, it's your turn to stand. Waiter—waiter, this gentleman wants another round of lagers."

This was the invariable end, and at closing time, having swung from the glory of newspaper proprietorship to the sordid penury of sharing out coppers in order to pay all bus fares home, we would walk along Cranbourn Street to Piccadilly Circus, and separate for the night.

THE BOOK-SHOPS OF BOHEMIA

THE BOOK-SHOPS OF BOHEMIA

WHERE the Charing Cross Road swirls up by the Hippodrome in a broad curve to Cambridge Circus and Oxford Street, it drops, for the short space of a few hundred yards, all shout and merriment and boisterous efflorescence of business, and becomes as sedate and proper an old street as ever exposed books on open stalls to the public fingers. The motor-buses may rattle up the middle of the road on their rollicking dance to Hampstead, the horse-pulled buses may swing and roll more slowly and nearer the gutter; no matter, for the pavements are quiet with learning and book-loving. All through the long summer afternoons, and in the winter, when the lamps hang over the shelves, books old, new, second and third hand, lie there in rows, waiting, these the stout old fellows, for Elias to carry them off under their arms; waiting, these the little ones, for other true book-lovers to pop them in their pockets. The little brown Oxford classics, the baby Virgil, the diminutive volumes of Horace and Catullus seem really to peak and shrivel on the shelves, suffocated in the open air, and longing, like townsmen for the town, for a snug square resting-place against the lining of a smoking coat. All about them are innumerable bound magazines, novels of Dickens, Scott, and Thackeray, novels of later times marked at half price, old sermons from sold vicarage libraries, old school grammars, and here and there the forgotten immortals of the nineties, essays published by Mr. John Lane, and poets with fantastic frontispieces. Against the window panes, behind the books, hang prints, Aubrey Beardsleys now, and designs by Housman and Nicholson, where once would Rowlandsons have hung, Bartolozzis, or perhaps an engraved portrait of Johnson or Goldsmith, done by Sir Joshua Reynolds, or perhaps again a selection of Amazing Beauties from the "Garland" or the "Keepsake" or the "Offering."

Summer and winter, book-buyers range up and down the street; book-buyers who mean to buy, book-buyers who would buy if they could, and book-buyers who have bought, and are now tormenting themselves by looking for bargains that they might have made, choicer than those they have already clinched. There is a rare joy in picking books from the stalls without the interference of any commercial fingers; a great content in turning over the pages of a book, a Cervantes perhaps, or a Boccaccio, or one of the eighteenth-century humourists, catching sight here and there of a remembered smile, and chuckling anew at the remembrance, putting the book down again, rather hurriedly, as if to decide once for all that you must not buy it, and then picking up another and repeating the performance. And then, the poignant, painful self-abandon when at last you are conquered, and a book leads you by the hand to the passionless little man inside the shop, and makes you pay him money, the symbol, mean, base, sordid in itself, but still the symbol, that the book has won, and swayed the pendulum of your emotions past the paying point.

I remember the buying of my "Anatomy of Melancholy" (that I have never read, nor ever mean to—I dare not risk the sweetness of the title); two big beautiful volumes, with a paper label on the back of each, they stood imperious on the shelves. I had seven-and-sixpence in the world, and was on my way up to Soho for dinner. I took one volume down, and turned the thick old leaves, and ran my eye over the black print, broken and patterned by quotations in italics, Latin quotations everywhere making the book a mosaic in two languages. To sit and smoke in front of such a book would be elysium. I could, of course, have got a copy at a library—but then I did not want to read it. I wanted to own it, to sit in front of it with a devotional mind, to let my tobacco smoke be its incense, to worship its magnificent name; and here it was in such a dress as kings and hierarchs among books should wear. If I were ever to have a Burton, this Burton would I have. I remember I laid the book down, and stoically lit a pipe, before daring to look at the flyleaf for the pencilled price. Just then another man, one with the air of riches, walked casually up to the stall, and, fearful for my prize and yet timorous of its cost, I seized it and turned with trembling fingers back to the beginning:

"Two vols. 8/-."

Turning my purse inside out, I went in, with the two volumes and the three half-crowns, to come to some agreement with the bookseller. He let me have the books, but dinner vanished for that night, as the meats from the table of Halfdan the Black, and I had to walk to Chelsea. But what a joyous walk that was in the early autumn evening. Those two heavy volumes one under each arm swung me up the hill from Piccadilly as if they had been magic wings. The feel of them on my sides sent my heart beating and my face into smiles. One of the volumes was uncut—UNCUT. My landlord met me at the door with my bill. "The Devil!" my heart said, "I will attend to it," uttered my lips; and upstairs, penniless, by the light of a candle, that is, after all, as Elia has it, "a kindlier luminary than sun or moon," I spent three hours cutting that volume, leaf by leaf, happier than can well be told.

There is something more real about this style of buying books than about the dull mercenary method of a new emporium. It is good, granted, to look about the shelves of a new bookshop, to see your successful friends and the authors you admire out-glittering each other in smart, gold-lettered, brilliant-coloured bindings; to pick up pretty little editions of your favourite books—what pretty ones there are nowadays, but how sad it is to see a staid old folio author compelled to trip it in a duodecimo——; all that is pleasant enough, but to spend money there is a sham and a fraud; it is like buying groceries instead of buying dreams.

And then, too, the people who buy in the ordinary shops are so disheartening. There is no spirit about them, no enthusiasm. You cannot sympathise with them over a disappointment nor smile your congratulations over a prize—they need neither. They are buying books for other people, not to read themselves. The books they buy are doomed, Christmas or birthday presents, to lie about on drawing-room tables. I am sorry for those people, but I am sorrier for the books. For a book is of its essence a talkative, companionable thing, or a meditative and wise; and think of the shackling monotony of life on a drawing-room table, unable to be garrulous, being uncut, and unable to be contemplative in the din of all that cackle.

The others, who deal at the second-hand shops, come there of a more laudable purpose, to buy books for themselves—or to sell them, if their libraries have become insufferably fuller than their purses. This last case is at once sorrowful and happy: sad for the heart pangs of playing the traitor to a book by handing it back to a bookseller, happy in that other people, perhaps you, perhaps I, have then a chance of buying it. It is an odd thing, by the way, that sumptuous volumes are always easiest to part with; a ragged, worn old thing, especially if it is small, tugs at our feelings, so that we cannot let it go, whereas a school prize or an elegant present—away with it. They say that little women are the longest loved. It is difficult for us to sympathise with Lord Tyrconnel, when in withdrawing his patronage from Richard Savage he alleged that, "having given him a collection of valuable books stamped with my own arms, I had the mortification to see them in a short time exposed to sale upon the stalls, it being usual with Mr. Savage, when he wanted a small sum, to take his books to the pawnbroker." How many presentation copies, in large paper and vellum, have not gone in a like manner? Though nowadays we deal direct with the bookseller, and do not soothe our consciences with the pretence of intended redemption that is possible when a pawnbroker receives the books.

This leads me conveniently to another subject. Many young authors find help towards a livelihood by selling the copies of new works that come to them for praise and blame from the newspapers. I remember, when first my

reviewing began, thinking it unfair to their writers thus to place books they had sent for nothing to the papers at once upon the second-hand stalls. But presently, as a Christmas season came on, and children's books and sensational novels poured in in their dozens and their twenties, the pile in the corner of my room grew beyond all bearing, for I would not insult the books that had been purchased in their own right by giving them these foundling newcomers as neighbours on the shelves. I was driven to reasoning again, and soon proved, with admirable comfortable logic, that an advertisement, or a piece of good advice, from so able a pen as my own must be worth more to an author than the chance sale of a copy on the stalls. I sent immediately for a bookseller, and from that time on he called each Monday to remove the mangled corpses of the week before. This practice, which is very generally adopted and makes a pleasant little addition to many meagre incomes, is the explanation of the quantities of glowing new novels and other books (some of them, to the discredit of the reviewing profession, uncut) that can be seen marked down to half or a third the published price in almost any book-shop in the Charing Cross Road. It is a temptation to buy the books of your friends in this easy way. I have often hesitated over a Masefield, or a Thomas, and the works of half a score of little poets. But God deliver me from such baseness.

These shops are not the stalls that delighted Lamb, and Gay before him. Those were farther east, some in Booksellers' Row, now cleared away by the improvements in the Strand, some in the neighbourhood of Covent Garden, some close by St. Paul's, where in the alleys round about a few such shops may still be found. The City shops were those that Gay describes:

> "Volumes on shelter'd stalls expanded lie,
> And various science lures the learned eye;
> The bending shelves with pond'rous scholiasts groan,
> And deep divines to modern shops unknown:
> Here, like the bee, that on industrious wing
> Collects the various odours of the spring,
> Walkers at leisure learning's flowers may spoil,
> Nor watch the wasting of the midnight oil.

> May morals snatch from Plutarch's tattered page,
> A mildew'd Bacon or Stagira's sage.
> Here saunt'ring 'prentices o'er Otway weep,
> O'er Congreve smile, or over D * * sleep."

Gay, walking "with sweet content on foot, wrapt in his virtue and a good surtout," the first covering perhaps being scanty enough, loved this impecunious public so much better than his own more opulent patrons that he prayed to his publisher, Bernard Lintot, "a great sputtering fellow," who must have been vastly annoyed at his author's unbusinesslike fancies:

> "O Lintot, let my labours obvious lie,
> Ranged on thy stall, for every curious eye;
> So shall the poor these precepts gratis know,
> And to my verse their future safeties owe."

Lamb loved them too. "There is a class of street readers," he says, "whom I can never contemplate without affection — the poor gentry, who, not having the wherewithal to buy or hire a book, filch a little learning at the open stall—the owner, with his hard eye, casting envious looks at them all the while, and thinking when they will have done. Venturing tenderly, page after page, expecting every moment when he shall interpose his interdict, and yet unable to deny themselves the gratification, they 'snatch a fearful joy!'"

Some of the older-fashioned stalls remain, but they are solitary. They do not sing together like the morning stars. They are isolated hermits, often in strange surroundings. In the open markets held in the shabbier streets, where flaring naphtha lights swing over barrows like those set up once a week in the squares of little country towns, I have often stood in the jostling crowd of marketers, to turn over old, greasy, tattered covers. There is an aloofness about the bookstall even there, where it stands in line with a load of brussels sprouts and cabbages on one side, and a man selling mussels and whelks on the other. The bookstall, even in its untidiness, has always the air of the gentleman of the three, come down in the world perhaps, but still one of a great family. I have sometimes been tempted to apologise to the bookseller for taking a penn'orth of cockles and vinegar while looking at his books. It seemed etiquette not to perceive that grosser, less intellectual stalls existed.

There are similar book barrows in the market streets of the East End, and some in Farringdon Street, where I have heard of bargains picked up for a song. But I have never visited them. There are good second-hand shops up the Edgeware Road, and I got Thorpe's "Northern Mythology" for three-pence in Praed Street. But my favourite of all the isolated shops is a queer little place at the dip of Bedford Street, where it drops into the Strand. It has but a lean row of books ranged on a narrow table in front of the window, but its prints are superb. There are maps some-times, and often old hand-coloured caricatures, figures with balloons full of jokes blowing from their mouths, hanging behind the glass or fluttering in the doorway. And, though the books are so few, I seldom pass the shop without seeing office boys from the Bedford Street or Henrietta Street offices skimming through them, now looking at one, now at another, until their tardy consciences hurry them at last upon their masters' errands.

Still, if we except Paternoster Row, mainly occupied by publishers, the Charing Cross Road is the only street whose character is wholly bookish. By these shops alone are there always a crowd of true bookmen. There are the clerks who bolt their lunches to be able to spend half an hour in glancing over books. There are reviewers selling newspaper copies. There are book-collectors watching for the one chance in ten thousand that brings a prize into the fourpenny box. There are book-lovers looking for the more frequent chance that brings them a good book at a little price, or lets them read it without buying it.

I have met old ladies there, with spectacles, and little bonnets with purple ribbons, eating buns before going back to the Museum to read, scanning over the bookshelves like birds pecking for crumbs over the cobbles. And sometimes I have met really old ladies, like Mrs. ——, who told me she had sat on Leigh Hunt's knee and put strawberries into his mouth; old ladies who remember the old days and the old bookshops, and come now to the Charing Cross Road for old sake's sake, just as a man reads over again a book that he read in his childhood for that reason alone. There was an old gentleman too, whom I loved to see striding across the street from shop to shop, dodging the buses as he crossed, with a long grey beard that divided at his chin and blew over his shoulders, and a huge coat, all brown fur without, that flapped about his legs. There was another too, with a white forehead and an absent eye, and thin black clothes with pockets bagged out by carrying libraries. I caught him once looking at a book upside down, deep in some dream or other: he came to himself suddenly, and saw that he had been observed—I loved him for the shame-faced, awkward way in which he tried to pretend he had been looking at a mark on the page. Then too there are young serious-faced poets, with who knows how many great works, ready planned, floating in the air about their heads: it is pleasant to watch the supercilious scorn with which they pass the shelves of lighter literature. It is delightful too, to see the learned young men from the country trying to hoodwink the bookseller, who really does not care, into thinking that they are of the connoisseurs, and in the know, by asking him with a particular air about special editions of Oscar Wilde, and who has the best collection of Beardsley drawings.

Nor must I forget the true Tom Folios,

who are "universal scholars as far as the title-pages of all authors, know the manuscripts in which they were discovered, the editions through which they have passed, with the praises or censures which they have received from the several members of the learned world. They think they give you an account of an author when they tell you the subject he treats of, the name of the editor, and the year in which it was printed." We have several such about the British Museum, and often they may be seen in the Charing Cross Road, picking over the older books, glancing at the title-pages (if by any chance you catch them looking at the text, be assured they are only examining the print). Some of them are useful fellows, like one I know, who, when he is in drink and merry, can give you a list of the half dozen best works on any subject you like to mention, with the libraries or bookshops where they may be found.

All these characters may be met by the bookstalls. Surely among the lot of them the books on those shelves have a better chance of finding their proper owners, the readers planned for them from their creation, than in any of the glass-fronted shops where the customers are harassed by extravagantly dressed young men, who assume, and usually rightly, that they know better what is wanted than the customers do themselves.

Indeed, I am quite with Gay in the matter. I would be happier to think of this book tattered and torn in a twopenny box than lying neat and uncut upon a drawing-room table. Therefore, O my publishers, though I cannot address you in neat verse like Mr. Gay's, let me pray you in plain honest prose —do send out a superabundance of copies to the newspapers, so that some at least may find their ignominious, happy way to the best and untidiest bookshops in the world.

OLD AND NEW FLEET STREET

OLD AND NEW FLEET STREET

JOHNSON and Boswell walked once in Greenwich Park, then very decent country, and even now no despicable imitation. "Is not this fine?" says the Doctor; Boswell answers, "Yes, sir; but not equal to Fleet Street"; and the Doctor clinches the matter with, "You are right, sir, you are right."

Indeed, Fleet Street, brave show as it is today, must have been splendid then, seen through old Temple Bar, a turning, narrow thoroughfare, with high-gabled houses a little overhanging the pavements, those pavements where crowds of gentlemen, frizzed and wigged, in coloured coats and knee-breeches, went to and fro about their business. There would come strutting little Goldsmith in the plum-coloured suit, and the sword so big that it seemed a pin and he a fly upon it. There would be Johnson, rolling in his gait, his vast stomach swinging before him, his huge laugh bellying out in the narrow street, with Boswell at his side, leaning round to see his face and catch each word as it fell from his lips. There would be Doctor Kenrick, Goldsmith's arch enemy, for whose fault he broke a stick over the back of bookseller Evans, and got a pummelling for his pains. There would be the usual mob of young fellows trying as gaily then as now to keep head above water by writing for the Press.

And then think of it in a later time, when Hazlitt walked those pavements, with straight, well-meant strides, as befits a man who has done his thirty miles a day along the Great North Road. Perhaps as he walked he would be composing his remarks on the oratory of the House of Commons, which he was engaged to report for Mr. Perry of the *Morning Chronicle*. Or perhaps, if it were Wednesday, he would turn in at Mitre Court, or meet a slim-legged, black-clothed figure with a beautiful head, Charles Lamb, coming out of the archway, or hurrying in there, with a folio under his arm, fresh from the stall of the second-hand bookseller. Perhaps Lamb might be playing the journalist himself, writing jokes for Dan Stuart of the *Morning Post*. You remember: "Somebody has said that to swallow six cross-buns daily consecutively for a fortnight would surfeit the stoutest digestion. But to have to furnish as many jokes daily, and that not for a fortnight, but for a long twelvemonth, as we were constrained to do, was a little harder exaction." Or perhaps you might meet Coleridge coming that way from his uncomfortable lodging in the office of the *Courier* up the Strand. Coleridge knew the ills of journalistic life. De Quincey "called on him daily and pitied his forlorn condition," and left us a description of his lodging. De Quincey had known worse himself, but this was evil enough. "There was no bell in the room, which for many months answered the double purpose of bedroom and sitting-room. Consequently I often saw him, picturesquely enveloped in nightcaps, surmounted by handkerchiefs endorsed upon handkerchiefs, shouting from the attics down three or four flights of stairs to a certain 'Mrs. Brainbridge,' his sole attendant, whose dwelling was in the subterranean regions of the house. There did I often see the philosopher, with the most lugubrious of faces, invoking with all his might this uncouth name of 'Brainbridge,' each syllable of which he intonated with long-drawn emphasis, in order to overpower the hostile hubbub coming downwards from the creaking press and the roar from the Strand which entered at all the front windows."

And then there was the Tom and Jerry time, when young bloods for sport came down at night to Temple Bar to overturn the boxes of the watchmen and startle their rheumatic occupants; when Reynolds would leave his insurance office to go to Jack Randall's in Chancery Lane to watch the sparring; when Pierce Egan, the first and greatest of sporting writers, would slip along the Strand from Soho for the same splendid purpose.

And then there was the time when Dickens,

a very young Bohemian, saw his first sketch, "called 'Mr. Minns and his Cousin'—dropped stealthily one evening at twilight, with fear and trembling, into a dark letter-box in a dark office up a dark court in Fleet Street—appear in all the glory of print."

And then, long before, there had been the magical Elizabethan Fleet Street, when Ben Jonson and his friends drank by Temple Bar, when Shakespeare met Falstaff and Pistol in the Fleet Street taverns, and was probably contemptuously cut by poor Greene, as "an upstart crow, beautified with our feathers, a puppet speaking from our mouths, an antick garnisht in our colours."

And now there are all these different Fleet Streets, one on the top of the other, dovetailed together indistinguishably. A building here, on old doorway there, the name of a side street, brings back a memory of one age or another. This tavern, for example, was given its name as a jest by a gay-dressed fellow in long locks, with a sword swinging at his side. There is the street of the White Friars. That building was designed by a subject of Queen Anne. Lamb walked past while those offices were still cradled in their scaffolding.

On a sunny morning there is no jollier sight in all the world than to look down Fleet Street, from a little below the corner of Fetter Lane on that side of the road. The thoroughfare is thronged with buses—green for Whitechapel, blue going to Waterloo Bridge, white

for Liverpool Street, gay old survivals of the coaching days, with their drivers windblown and cheerfully discontented, the healthiest-looking fellows, who would once have driven four-in-hand, and are too soon to vanish and be replaced by uniformed chauffeurs. Already the great motor-buses whirl past them down the narrow street, and dwarf them by their size. There goes a scarlet mail wagon, there a big dark van from some publishers up Paternoster Row. Barrows creep along the gutter, some selling chocolates "for an advertisement," at a penny a stick, some selling bananas, "two for 1½d.," the penny written big, and the halfpenny as small and apparently insignificant as is consistent with street-selling honesty. The toot-toot of a motor bicycle worries among the other noises like the yap of a terrier, and a boy swings past, round the backs of the buses, twisting his way under the horses' noses with devilish enjoyment, a huge sack of newspapers fastened on his back.

On either side, above all the flood of traffic, stand the tall narrow houses, and the larger newer buildings, with the names of newspapers and magazines blazoned in brilliant gold and colour across wall and window. The sunlight, falling across the street, leaves one side in shadow, and lights the other with a vivid glare, as if to make the shadowed side as jealous as it can. Men and women hurry on the pavements: typewriter girls, office boys, news editors, reporters, writers, and artists in pen and ink jostling each other down the street. And if you look up from the noise and movement, you see the grey dome of St. Paul's, standing aloof, immutable, at the top of Ludgate Hill. How many times has the sun shone on that great pile of stone, how many lives have been hurried through within sight of its majesty and calm! How many men yet will untidily live out their days, harassed, nervous, never giving a moment but to the moment itself, while that massive building rises as if in the sky, a monument of peace above the tumult!

As you watch the people on the pavements you will gradually learn to distinguish by their manner of walking the men who pass you by. There are the young fellows who walk as hard as if the world depended on the rapid accomplishment of their business; these are the men who do not matter, who seek to hide their unimportance from themselves. The real editor of a successful paper walks with less show of haste, an easier tread, a less undignified scramble. He knows the time he may allow, and is never in a hurry. It is his subordinates, the fledglings of the Press, and the editors of small unsuccessful rags, who are always, as we north countrymen say, in a scrow. Poor fellows! Fleet Street life is so heartless, so continuous: they must do something, or it would not know that they are there.

Then there are the writers and illustrators, men of a less regular stamp, men whom it is difficult to imagine sitting at an office desk, men who walk at their own pace, and look into the shop windows, men who make of their walk a lazy kind of essay, with all manner of digressions. These are the unattached, the free lances, who know that the papers for which they write cannot do without them (it is extraordinary, though, how soon the feat is accomplished if they happen to die), and in that proud knowledge saunter down to shake the editors by the hand, and ask what is to be the game this week, or to suggest some topic of their own. There will be Chesterton, Ursa Major Redivivus, rolling with an armful of papers from side to side of the pavement, cannoning from astounded little man into astounded little man, and chuckling all the time at one or other of the half dozen articles that he is making inside that monstrous head. There will be Bart Kennedy, a massive, large-built fellow, walking the pavement with the air prescribed by the best of drill sergeants, "as if one side of the street belonged to him, and he expected the other shortly." There will be the critic from the country, striding down Bouverie Street to see what impertinent poets have dared to send their books to his paper for review. There a little dark-faced writer of short stories, an opulent manufacturer of serial tales, a sad-looking maker of humorous sketches, and a dexterous twister of political jokes into the elaborate French metres that make a plain statement look funny. There will be twenty more.

As you walk down the street you realise how impossible it is to throw off the consciousness of its ancient history. Over the way is Mitre Court, where Lamb's friends met on Wednesdays, and discussed "Of Persons One would wish to have Seen." How impossible it was even then appears from the fact that Chaucer's name was suggested to the Mitre Courtiers by some one asking whether they could not "see from the window the Temple Walk in which old Chaucer used to take his exercise."

Farther down there is an alley-way leading to Salisbury Court, where Richardson ran his printing business, and built the house that his wife did not like, and wrote his interminable books. In the alley-way is the tavern where at the present day the Antient Society of Cogers meet to discuss the world and its affairs.

They used to meet at the Green Dragon round the corner, in Fleet Street again.

Farther up, at the top of the street, close by Temple Bar, there is the Cock, an admirable place, where you are still fed in high-backed pews and served by English waiters. Tennyson was so delighted by one of them that he wrote "Will Waterproof's Lyrical Monologue," from which I filch some livening verses:

> "Oh, plump headwaiter at the Cock,
> To which I most resort,
> How goes the time? 'Tis five o'clock,
> Go fetch a pint of port.
> And let it not be such as that
> You set before chance comers,
> But such whose father grape grew fat
> On Lusitanian summers.
>
> The Muse, the jolly Muse it is!
> She answered to my call,
> She changes with that mood or this,
> Is all in all to all:

She lit the spark within my throat,
To make my blood run quicker,
Used all her fiery will, and smote
Her life into the liquor.

And hence this halo lives about
The waiter's hands, that reach
To each his perfect pint of stout,
His proper chop to each.
He looks not like the common breed
That with the napkin dally;
I think he came, like Ganymede,
From some delightful valley.

The Cock was of a larger egg
Than modern poultry drop,
Step'd forward on a firmer leg,
And cram'd a plumper crop;
Upon an ampler dunghill trod,
Crow'd lustier late and early,
Sipt wine from silver, praising God,
And raked in golden barley.

A private life was all his joy,
Till in a court he saw
A something-pottle-bodied boy
That knuckled at the taw;
He stoop'd and clutch'd him, fair and good,
Flew over roof and casement;
His brothers of the weather stood
Stock still for sheer amazement.

But he, by farmstead, thorpe, and spire,
And follow'd with acclaims,
A sign to many a staring shire
Came crowing over Thames.
Right down by smoky Paul's they bore,
Till, where the street grows straiter,
One fix'd for ever at the door,
And one became head-waiter."

It reads as if he had enjoyed the place. The Cock is still above the door, and it is not impossible to believe that these waiters, like that one, were brought in a manner of their own from some hidden valley where the napkin is the laurel of ambition, where men are born waiters as others are born priests or kings.

Pepys loved the Cock: "eat a lobster here, and sang and was mighty merry." Johnson knew it too. The tavern has been rebuilt, though all the old fittings are retained, and every day from half-past twelve till three its dark square pews are full of talking, feeding men, as in the older days.

Far down on the Fetter Lane side of the street there is the Cheshire Cheese, still the dirty-fronted, low-browed tavern, with stone flasks in the window, that it was even before Johnson's time. Here, so people say, Johnson and Goldsmith used to sup and be merry with their friends. Perhaps it was the haunt of one of the talking clubs of which neither of them was ever tired. Although it is nowhere written that Johnson crossed the threshold, it is very unlikely that the man who asserted that "a tavern chair was the throne of human felicity" could have neglected such an opportunity as was his. For he lived for some time in Wine Office Court, in whose narrow passage is the entrance to the tavern, and I doubt if he could have passed it every day without finding some reason for encouraging it. Indeed, with Macaulayic logic, they show you Johnson's corner seat, the wall behind it rubbed smooth by the broadcloth of innumerable visitors, "to witness if they lie." It is a pleasant brown room, this, in the tavern, with Johnson's portrait hanging on the wall, old wooden benches beside good solid tables, and a homely smell of ale and toasted cheese. Here many of the best known journalists make a practice of dining, and doubtless get some sauce of amusement with their meat from the young men and girls, literary and pictorial, destined to work for the cheap magazines and fashion papers, who always begin their professional career by visiting the Cheshire Cheese for inspiration. Up a winding, crooked, dark staircase there are other rooms, with long tables in them stained with wine and ale, and in one of them the Rhymers' Club used to meet, to drink from tankards, smoke clay pipes, and recite their own poetry.

In the passage into Wine Office Court, almost opposite the narrow entry of the Cheshire Cheese, there is a door set back, that denies admittance (in big printed letters) to all but members of the Press Club. This is a sort of substitute for the coffee-houses of the eighteenth century. Goldsmith used to gather suggestions for the *Bee* at "The Temple Exchange Coffee House near Temple Bar"; and in the fourth number of that ill-fated periodical he confessed that he was tempted:

"To throw off all connexions with taste, and fairly address my countrymen in the same engaging style and manner with other periodical pamphlets much more in vogue than probably mine shall ever be. To effect this, I had thought of changing the title into that of *The Royal Bee*, *The Anti-Gallican Bee*, or *The Bee's Magazine*. I had laid in a stock of popular topics, such as encomiums on the King of Prussia, invective against the Queen of Hungary and the French, the necessity of a militia, our undoubted sovereignty of the seas, reflections upon the present state of affairs, a dissertation upon liberty, some seasonable thoughts upon the intended bridge of Blackfriars, and an address to Britons; the history of an old woman whose teeth grew three inches long, an ode upon our victories, a rebus, an acrostic upon Miss Peggy P., and a journal of the weather. All this, together with four extraordinary pages of letterpress, a beautiful map of England, and two prints curiously coloured from nature, I fancied might touch their very souls."

Reading that is like listening to plans laid down a hundred times a year in the Press Club smoking-room. There are the members, their legs hung elegantly over the backs of chairs, cigars, briars, or meerschaums between their teeth, glasses of whisky on the small round tables at their sides, planning their baits for the British public much as anglers observe the sky, and decide between the likely merits of different artificial flies. The prints "curiously coloured from nature" have still their votaries.

"A good three-colour plate, that's the very thing"—I can hear the tones of the conspirator's voice. Reverse Goldsmith's popular politics, abuse Germany, fling in a black-and-white cartoon of a fat John Bull kissing a short-skirted French demoiselle, with a poem about the *entente cordiale*, substitute Labour Party for liberty—the picture is the life.

The Press Club is a great manufactory of comfortable fame. It hangs caricatures of its members round its walls. A man who sees his own caricature has a foretaste of immortality, and of this flattery the Club is generous to itself. And you cannot ask a member what such a one of his fellows does without being made to feel ashamed of your ignorance of his celebrity. With a cold shock you learn that you have fallen behind the times, and that men are famous now of whom you never heard.

As well as the Press Restaurant, and the more noted taverns, there are plenty of places up and down the street where famous men can get their beef and beer like ordinary people; but the most entertaining places of refreshment are two small cafés that are exactly similar to many in other parts of the town. At the top of Bouverie Street there is a little white-painted, gold-lettered shop, with cakes and pastries in the window. You go in there, and find rows of chocolate-coloured marble table-tops, standing on moulded iron legs, and surrounded by cheap wooden chairs. There are mirrors on all the walls, which are hung with notices that tell of the price of Bovril by the cup, or the cost of a pound packet of special coffee. Girls, dressed in black, with peaked white caps and spotless aprons, scuttle about with trays, and cloths to mop up the tea which previous customers have spilt. You may go downstairs into a yellow atmosphere of smoke and electric light, and find another room, full of tables like the first, where crowds of young men are drinking tea and playing chess. If you sit down here, and ask knowingly to have the moisture wiped off before you lay your book on the table, and then have buttered toast and tea brought you by the white-capped girl, and finally throw the food into yourself as if by accident while you read your book; if you do all these things as if you were born to it, why then you may feel yourself the equal of any journalist in the place.

The other little café is on the opposite side of the street, close by Fetter Lane. A green, elaborately fronted shop, it is slightly more expensive than the first, and more luxurious. The tables hide their innocence under white cloths, and you are not given the satisfaction of watching the swabbing up of the last customer's tea. There is a string band playing in a recess. If you wish to see real live journalists, you may see them here drinking black coffee out of little cups in the mildest possible manner.

This chapter is long already, and a little unruly in digression, but I cannot conclude it without mentioning one of the innumerable talking clubs that meet at the taverns in the neighbourhood, just as Goldsmith's friends used to meet on Wednesdays at the Globe, and for the same purpose. I was introduced to it soon after coming into Bohemia. There was a long table down the middle of the room, and round it, on benches, were seated about a dozen men, some young, some very young, few over thirty, with beer mugs and spirit glasses before them, and pipes in their mouths. The room already reeked of the good, dirty, homely smell of tobacco smoke, although they had but just assembled. There was a big cigar box at one end of the table, into which each member dropped a coin representing the amount of liquor he expected to drink during the evening, and the amount he thought fitting for any guest he had happened to bring. A huge snuff box was passed round at intervals. All the members took pinches, and sneezed immediately afterwards, with apparent enjoyment. There was a fierce argument in progress when we came in. One of the members had just published a book, and the others were attacking his as healthy wolves worry a lame one. "What do you mean by this in the chapter on Swinburne?"——"I think you're a little mistaken in saying this about Raphael"——"Swinburne has ceased to count anyway"——"Who dared say that Swinburne has ceased to count?"——"Swinburne's poetry will last as long as Victor Hugo's, and Hugo is the greatest of the nineteenth century"——"Hugo, Pfa! a meteor flash, no more . . . a careless fellow . . . But the question of French poetry

is interesting enough"——"Ah! French poetry . . ." Half the company turned on the last speaker, and the poor author, who had been waiting to answer his critics, took a drink of beer, filled his pipe, and smiled to himself. French poetry as matter for discussion led them to Villon, and from Villon they passed to the question of capital punishment for trivial offences, and from that to the question whether capital punishment is justifiable at all. At this there was a cry of faddism, which introduced an argument about Mr. Bernard Shaw. The evening, typical of many others in Fleet Street, passed like magic, as the talk swung from subject to subject, and the tankards were emptied and refilled, and the snuffbox made its rounds.

SOME NEWSPAPERS AND MAGAZINES

SOME NEWSPAPERS AND MAGAZINES

I MENTIONED a little newspaper that, by its payments for my young essays and exuberantly juvenile reviews, made it possible for me to adventure by myself and take my first lodging in Chelsea. It was a good example of those obscure, high-hearted little rags that keep alive so many of the unknown writers, and help so many youthful critics to deceive themselves into self-congratulation at the sight of their own names in capital letters. Your name in capital letters at the foot of a review seems as permanent, as considerable a memorial as the dome of St. Paul's. It is impossible to imagine it forgotten. Indeed, there have been plenty of people surprised by their first glad printed outbursts into contented silence for the rest of their lives. For them, their doings have been for ever consecrated from those of the herd by the memory of that great Saturday long ago when their names flaunted it upon a Fleet Street poster. Their air of "having been through all that" is very delightful.

The little paper was published once a week as an organ of sane Liberal opinion and enlightened criticism (I quote from memory of its prospectus.) It had offices and a brass door-plate in a street off the eastern end of the Strand. Well I remember the thrill of passing that door-plate as a regular contributor. Surely, surely, I thought, all the street must know that I was I, the I whose articles were, well, not the best in the paper, but certainly among the pleasantest. I used to glance both ways along the pavement, before plunging in on Tuesday afternoon to learn, as a privileged counsellor, what we were to announce to the world on the following Saturday.

Up three pair of stairs I used to stamp, quite noisily, perhaps with half an idea of further establishing my self-confidence; for always, in those early days, I nursed a secret fear that each article would be the last, that on the next Tuesday the editor would frown upon my suggestions, and firmly dismiss me from his employ.

How groundless was my fear: this editor could never have brought himself to dismiss any one. When he engaged new contributors, instead of dismissing the old, he used to swell the paper to make room for them, without, alas! increasing the circulation. It grew from eight to twelve pages, from twelve to sixteen, from sixteen, with a triumphant announcement on its solitary poster, that was pasted by the editor himself, when nobody was looking, on a hoarding outside the office, to a magnificent twenty. There it rested; not because its editor had grown flint of heart, but because he had grown light of purse, and been compelled to cede the publication to another.

He was the most charming editor I ever met. A little out of breath after the three pair of stairs, I would swing through the long attic that was piled waist-high with the past issues of the moribund little periodical, through the "ante-room," a small scrubby hole partitioned from the attic, and furnished with an old cane-bottomed chair for the use of visitors, to be greeted by a glad and boyish shout from the chief himself. An eager-faced, visionary little man, he lolled in an expensive swing chair before an expensive roll-top desk, both obviously bought in the first flush of editorial dignity. A cigarette in a patent holder stuck jauntily between his teeth, and a pile of white unwritten paper stood before him on his blotting pad. It was delightful to see the unaffected joy of him at the excuse my arrival afforded him for talking instead of writing.

"Was he busy?" I would mischievously ask. "Had I not better disturb him another time?"

"Yes, he was busy, always busy; but," and here he would hurriedly scuffle all his papers into the back of the desk, and close his fountain pen, "he held it the first duty of an editor to be ready to listen to the ideas of his contributors"; and then, dear fellow, he would talk without stopping until, after perhaps a couple of hours of wide, of philanthropic conversation, in which he took all sides and argued all opinions with equal skill, I would venture to introduce, as a little thing that scarce deserved a place in such a talk, the subject of work and the week's issue of the paper. He would sober instantly and sadly, like a spaniel checked in mid career. "Well, what is it you want to write? An article on prettiness in literature. Do it, my good chap, do it. I concur heartily in all your views. Prettiness in literature is an insipid, an effeminate, a damnable, despicable thing. Oh —I see—you intend rather to show its merits. Yes, yes; very true indeed. He would surely be a mean-souled creature who would ask for a coarser dish. Prettiness in literature, delicacy, daintiness, poetry, the very flower of our age, the whitebait of the literary dinner. Certainly, young man, certainly; a column and a half, by all means." And then, after I had asked for and obtained a few books for review (classics if possible, for they were at the same time education and a source of profit), he would rattle off again into his flowery talk of the reformation of the world, that must take its beginning in the heart of man, of a scheme for working men's clubs, of a project for turning Socialists into sane Liberals, such as would be regular buyers of the little paper, and so on, and so on, ending up always with the same exhortation: "My dear young fellow, do smoke cigarettes instead of that dirty cess-pot of a pipe. Consider: with a cigarette you destroy your instrument, the paper tube, with each enjoyment. Whereas with the thing you smoke, you use it until it is saturated with iniquity and become a very still of poisonous vapours. Well, well, good after-noon. Let me have the article on Thursday morning, and come and see me again next Tuesday."

That was in the early days of my connec-tion with him. But after a few months I was admitted a member of the chosen band who met on Thursday morning, and, with paper and ink provided free, lay prone on the back numbers in the long attic, and practi-cally wrote the whole paper, improving the work of other contributors, curtailing their articles, filling them up with jokes or paren-theses, till they swelled or shrank to the re-quired space, and in their own special columns, over their own names, instructed the universe on everything under heaven, and sometimes made metaphysical excursions even there.

We used to meet at three after a Soho or Fleet Street lunch, and wrote continuously until we fell asleep, or until the work was done. The office boy, who loved these days because on them we made a point of calling him Mr. Sub-Editor, went whistling to and fro, carrying big envelopes to the printers round the corner, and bearing mighty jugs of beer, from the tavern a few doors off, to the perspiring men of genius who lay and laughed and toiled on the waste of dusty back numbers in the attic room.

It was a spirited little paper. We used to attack everybody who was famous, excepting only Mr. Kipling, Mr. Sturge Moore, Mr. Yeats, and Mr. Laurence Binyon. Each of these four had his passionate admirers on the staff, and was consequently exempt from criticism. We had a gay way with any writer on whose merits we had no decided opinions. Two of us would put our heads together, and the one write a eulogium, the other a violent attack. One would exalt him as a great contributor to English literature, the other jeer at him as a Grub Street hack. The two reviews, numbered one and two, would be published side by side It was an entertaining, admirable system. In matters other than literature we had our fling at everybody. except the select, the very select few to whom our editor attributed the mysterious "sane Liberalism" with which he was himself inspired. But our happiest moments were when one of our company had written a book. We were all young and all ambitious. The most energetic and diplomatic of us contrived to coax a publisher into issuing one book, or even two, every year, and, of course, we looked to our own organ for a vigorous backing. We got it. On the day of publication would appear large-typed, efflorescent articles, headed "At Last a Novelist," or "A Second

Balzac," or "An Essayist of Genius," or "The True Spirit in Poetry," and one of the staff would redden with pleasure as he read the article that referred to him, and wonder if this miraculous, this precocious, prodigious, world-shaking genius were indeed himself.

Alas! I doubt whether any article of ours ever sold a single book, for we had no circulation. Indeed, so notorious did our non-success become, even among ourselves, though we discreetly tried to veil our knowledge from each other, that when the editor had arranged with three new poets, whom I did not know by sight, to write poetry for us, and I saw a man in a coffee-house reading the paper, I went boldly up to him and asked, "Are you Mr. So-and-So, Mr. So-and-So, or Mr. So-and-So?"

"I am not," he replied.

"Do you mean to say you bought that paper and are not a contributor to it?" The thing was a miracle.

He actually had, and it was so delightful to find any one outside ourselves who read what we had written, that I made friends with him at once, and have remained in friendship with him ever since. But I believe he was the only one.

It was natural that the editor, who was also the proprietor, should at last be compelled to abandon a paper so meanly supported. The man who took it over made a different thing of it. Its youth and jollity and energy were left behind, and it did its best to become a staid paper of the world. The new editor was of those Hazlitt classed as "a sort of tittle-tattle—difficult to deal with, dangerous to discuss." He disliked all suggestion that had not come from himself. It was necessary, if an idea were to be adopted, to flatter him into thinking it his own. I never knew him write an amusing thing, and I only once heard him say one, and then it was by accident. He had assembled us, and announced that in future we should not be allowed to sign our articles. The very joy of life was gone, but he said he wanted the paper to have an individual personality. We protested, and he replied quite seriously: "That is all very well. But if all you fellows sign your articles, what becomes of *my* personality?" I forgave him everything for that.

This is not a chapter on newspaper editors, but I cannot go on to talk of magazines without paying some tribute to the ingenious adventurers who, more successful than those two, manage to keep their little rags afloat. It is amazing how many small papers, without any circulation, are yet published week by week. The secret history of the struggles with the printers, who insolently refuse to work when their bills are too long overdue, and the battles with the contributors, who prefer to be paid than otherwise, is as entertaining as the intrigues of courtiers to save themselves from downfall and disgrace.

There is a story in Fleet Street now about a little paper devoted to mild reform—vegetarianism, no cruelty to dogs, anti-vaccinationism, and the like—whose editor managed to keep the paper and himself alive on subsidies from religious faddists. From his office at the end of an alley he could see his visitors before they arrived, and when he saw a likely victim in some black-coated righteous old gentleman, he opened a Bible and laid it on his desk. Then he knelt down at his chair. When the old gentleman had climbed the stairs, and had inquired for him of the office boy, he heard from the inner room a solemn, earnest voice: "O Lord, soften Thou the heart of some rich man, that of his plenty he may give us wherewithal to carry on the good work that this small paper does in Thy name . . ." and so on. He would lift a finger to the boy. "Hush!" he would say; "your master is a good man," and presently going in, when the prayer was ended, would write out a cheque at least as liberal as it was ill-deserved.

The *Jonquil* is a famous example. It was edited by a man called Beldens, who had a little money, but not much. He contrived to retain his writers by a most ingenious appeal to their gambling instincts. Every Saturday all the cheques were accurately made out and delivered to the contributors. But these soon found that there was never more money to the credit of the paper in the bank than would pay the first three or four of the cheques presented. The rest were returned dishonoured. The result was not unamusing, for Beldens had chosen a bank in Fulham, while his office was in Covent Garden. Every Saturday at the appointed time all the contributors used to attend, with hansoms, specially chosen for the fleetness of their horses, waiting in a row outside. Beldens would come, smiling and urbane, into the outer office, with the bundles of little pink slips. As soon as they had been passed round there would be a wild scuffle of genius on the stairs, the dishevelled staff would rush out of the door, leap into their hansoms, and race pell mell for the bank, the fortunate first arrivals dividing with their cabbies the moneys that their respective efficiencies had achieved.

* * * * *

The larger newspapers, and the popular monthlies, are not important in Bohemia, except as means of earning money or getting on in the world. We flatter ourselves that they would be dull without us, but their life is not ours. The periodicals that really matter to us are of a different kind, and we run them ourselves. They are quarterlies, or annuals, never perennials Few survive three issues, and those that live long do no honour to their old age. For the glory of these papers is their youth. A dozen names spring to mind: *The Yellow Book*, *The Savoy*, *The Pageant*, all of the time when Arthur Symons, Aubrey Beardsley, Max Beerbohm, Frederick Wedmore, were not yet known and discussed by the laggard public; *The Butterfly*, *The Dial* of Shannon and Ricketts, *The Dome* of Laurence Housman, W. B. Yeats, Laurence Binyon, and another brood of writers; down to *The Venture*, that lived two years, 1904 and 1905, and then died like the rest. And at the present moment at least three new dreams are being crystallised into the disillusionment of print, and will appear and fail next year.

These magazines are not like the "Literary Souvenirs" and the pocket books of the early nineteenth century, to which they have been often compared. They have no delicious little engravings by popular artists of lovers reading books together, nor are they full of "pieces" of prose and verse collected from the most obliging of the well-known authors of their day. They are written and illustrated by men more famous in Bohemia than elsewhere. Bohemia is the one country whose prophets find most honour at home. They are read lovingly by their writers, looked at by their illustrators, and discussed by all the crowd of young women who, by dressing in green gowns without collars, wearing embroidered yokes, scorning the *Daily Mail*, and following the fortunes of the studios, keep in the forefront of literary and artistic progress.

The Germ is the original of all these undertakings. From time to time a set of young men, like the Pre-Raphaelites, grow beyond the stage of sedulous aping, and find that they are producing something in literature and art that, not being a facile imitation of an established mode, is difficult to sell. They want a hearing, and find their pictures refused by the exhibitions as insults to the traditions of art, and their poems and stories rejected by the ordinary magazines and reviews as incomprehensible rubbish. Half a dozen poets, painters, and prosemen put their heads together, and plan a magazine that is not to be as others, gross, vapid, servile to a vulgar or sentimental taste, but a sword to cut upwards through the conventional fog to the brightness and glory of a new constellation of ideals. You must be one of them to appreciate their pictures, and have read what they have read to enjoy their writings. They hear "different drummers," and all who are not for them are against them. It is in such ventures that the men who are later to be accepted with applause make their first appearance. "The Blessed Damozel" was published in *The Germ* when few knew anything of the Pre-Raphaelites. *The Germ* was a commercial failure, but who has not heard of Rossetti?

Few printed things are more delightful or

more troublesome to produce than one of these free-lance miscellanies. The editors (there is usually a committee of at least three) go about in pride, conscious of the vitality of their movement, scornful of popular ignorance, and hopeful in their secret hearts that they are making history as others did before them. They carry with them through the studios the glorious feeling that "there is something in the air." They spend whole nights planning together, examining a dozen different kinds of papers, to find one suitable alike for blocks and text, comparing specimens from twenty printers. All is pleasant for them until their friends, outside the particular set that work together and believe in each other, begin to offer contributions. It is a difficult thing to tell a man that his work is not good enough, when he is no younger than yourself; it is an insult to suggest that he belongs to an older school, that his is a dying day, and that you cannot join the evening and the morning lights in this paper of yours that is to represent the dawn. But it must be done; and it is likely that thenceforth there is a studio you must not visit, an injured man whom you must skilfully avoid in taking your place at the Soho dinner-tables.

That is one of the difficulties; another, even more serious, is of finance. It is a sad thing that financiers are not often constructed like poets, eager to spill their best for the sweetness and joy of spilling it. It is hard that a man of money can seldom be persuaded to run a magazine except with a view to material profit. Even if the enhanced price of *The Germ* makes him think that another Garland of Youth, another Miscellany sounding another bugle, will, if better advertised, pay (loathsome word!) from the first, he assumes command of your fair vision, as if of a department store, inserts some terrible verses by a friend of his, and turns your dream to dust before your eyes. I was connected with one such performance, run for sordid gain by a financier, and it was a miserable affair. The stupid fellow saw money in poetry and pictures, as he might have seen it in corn or beef. He knew nothing, and it was as if the magazine had been edited by a five shilling piece. Each new contributor that he enrolled spun him in a new direction. One suggested a second, and the second suggested a third, so that the prose, the poetry, and the pictures sounded the whole gamut of intellectual notes, and the original projectors retired in disgust, to the financier's surprise. Of all such magazines, as he ruefully claimed for it, it was the most varied. It was also the least successful. It represented money instead of youth.

No; you have not only to catch your financier, but to tame him. He must understand that he is no more than the means to the end, and be proud of his subjection, happy never to see his money again, and content to have contributed his insignificant aid to the progress of literature and art. When such a man is discovered, which is not often, there is joy in Bohemia. The models, gossiping as they go, carry the great news. In a dozen studios men paint as their caprice takes them, and in a dozen lodgings imps of freedom ride a dozen pens. The shackles are off at last, that is the cry, and something fresh and extravagant is the result, something that overshoots the mark by its own vigour, but shows by its direction that there is a mark to be shot at, at which people have not aimed before.

WAYS AND MEANS

WAYS AND MEANS

A LITTLE time ago there was a great outcry against what was called "literary ghosting," a fraudulent passing off of the work of unknown writers under more famous names. There was a correspondence in a literary paper that betrayed how novels were written in the rough by inexperienced hands under the guidance of hardened manufacturers of serials; and, indeed, when we consider only how many prominent athletes of no particular literary ability are able to publish books on their profession, it is obvious that a good deal of this kind of business must be done. Indeed, in one form or another, ghosting is one of the usual ways by which the unfortunate young writer sustains himself in Grub Street, or Bohemia, or whatever else you like to call that indefinite country where big longings and high hopes are matched by short purposes and present discomforts.

Many a man has been saved from what seemed a descent into the drudgeries of clerkship by the different drudgery of writing, say, the reminiscences of an admiral, the history of a parish, or innumerable short reviews, for which other people got the credit. And Richard Savage, in his witty pamphlet called "An Author to be Let," betrays that the abuse is not only of our day. Iscariot Hackney of that book confesses that:

"Many a time I wrote obscenity and profaneness, under the names of Pope or Swift. Sometimes I was Mr. Joseph Gay, and at others Theory Burnet, or Addison. I abridged histories and travels, translated from the French what they never wrote, and was expert at finding out new titles for old books. When a notorious thief was hanged, I was the Plutarch to preserve his memory; and when a great man died, mine were his Remains, and mine the account of his last will and testament." That is the whole trade put in a paragraph.

Nowadays the matter has been reduced to system. There are men who are paid to write all the reviews in a paper, and farm out the work piecemeal, or even get ambitious boys and girls to do it for them, by way of apprenticeship, paying them a meagre wage. There are agents who make a living by supplying ghost-written books to publishers who keep up for appearance sake the pretence of not being in the know. They get their twenty, forty, fifty pounds a volume, and have them written by impecunious Bohemians to whom they pay the weekly salary of a junior clerk. Here is a true account of a youthful ghost.

He was a poet, and in those days a bad one. He carried more poor verses than good money in his pocket. And one day, when he had little more than a few coppers and some penny stamps, he happened to see an advertisement for "a young and experienced writer with a thorough knowledge of athletics." He kept the appointment suggested by the newspaper, and found a mean house in one of the southern suburbs. A herd of lean fellows were waiting in a dirty passage, and presently a cheerful business-like little man came out, and chose him with one companion as the likeliest-looking of the lot. They were set to write, at tables in the corners of an undusted, cat-haunted room, specimen chapters of a book on croquet. They were both appointed, and the other man, an old hand, borrowed five shillings in advance. Next day, when the young fellow arrived in the morning, he found that his colleague was there before him, drunk, holding the garden railings, and shouting blasphemies at a bedraggled cat that slunk about the waste scrap of ground behind them. The agent held up the drunkard to him as a warning, told him that sobriety was the spirit of success, and that, as he had the job to himself, he would be allowed to gain extra experience by doing the other man's work as well as his own. He was young, enthusiastic, glad to have an opportunity of working at all. In two months he had finished six books, that still annoy him by showing their bright-lettered covers on the railway bookstalls. He wrote on an average between two and four thousand words a day. At last, one day when he was working in an upper room of the agent's house, the little creature came upstairs and saw fit to congratulate him. "You are doing very well indeed," he said, "for one so unaccustomed to literary labour." That brought an end to the engagement. He left immediately, lest he should be unable to refrain from throwing an inkpot at the agent's head. It is in its way rather fun to be suddenly an authority on subjects of which you knew nothing till you sat down to write about them. And it is very good practice in journalism—though it is always easier to write when you are ignorant than when you know too much; you have a freer hand. But for a poet to hear such work called literary labour! That was too much. He never returned, and the agent was left sorrowing for the loss of an industrious hack.

Of course, the young man, you will say, should never have stooped to such work. He ought to have borrowed, or persuaded his landlady to let him live until his good luck should bring the settlement of her bills. But he could not borrow. There are some unfortunates who cannot; I hate borrowing myself. And it is an awful thing to be without money and miserably afraid of tiding over evil straits on somebody else's. Some there are, brave, high-souled fellows, who could borrow the world to play at ball, and never feel the responsibility, whereas others are uneasy and not themselves with a single shilling that does not belong to them. Some seem to live on credit as naturally as they breathe, and I remember the surprise of one of these: "What! You don't owe anybody anything! Good Lord! man, lend me half a sovereign."

People who by some misfortune of nature are unable to risk dishonesty by borrowing without having certain means of repayment are reduced to all kinds of unhappy expedients, and sometimes even to dying, like poor Chatterton,* in order to make both ends meet. Of him Johnson could say, "This is the most extraordinary young man that has encountered my knowledge. It is wonderful how the whelp has written such things," and yet, after three months' fight among the papers, living on almost nothing, and writing home to his people brave proud letters about his success, to keep them from anxiety, he spent three days without food, and then killed himself with arsenic, rather than accept from a landlady the food for which he doubted his ability to repay her. The most terrible detail in the tragedy was the memorandum that lay near him when he died, and showed that over ten pounds were owed him by his publishers. Ah me, in the days when I read that story ten pounds seemed opulence for a lifetime. It seemed a cruel and impossible thing, as all cruelty seems when we are young, that one who was owed so much should yet starve into suicide.

* In Brook Street, Holborn.

That is one of the worst hardships of painter or writer. His money, even when earned, is as intangible as the dawn. It is gold, but he may not handle it; real, but a dream. He must live, while he does his work, on air, and then, when the picture hangs in the drawing-room of the purchaser, and the article has been printed, published, and forgotten, he must wait, perhaps for months, perhaps for years, and sometimes indeed until he is passed into another world where he can have no opportunity of spending it, for the money that is his. It is not until he is a success, or at least no longer an anonymous Bohemian, that his money is paid in advance, or upon the completion of his labour. Little wonder that when at last it comes, it comes as a surprise, and sends him gaily into bright extravagance that leaves him with a purse as empty as before.

I have heard people say that all the wild, irregular struggle for existence that was known by Goldsmith, by Johnson, by old Roberto Greene, has faded away from the literary life. They say that now, young men, top-hatted, frock-coated, enter the offices of newspapers, earn comfortable salaries, write their novels or whatever they may be in their spare hours, and arrive, neat, unruffled as Civil Servants, by mere process of time at their success. It is not so. "Once a sub-editor always a sub-editor," said a very successful one, who had given up hope of succeeding at anything else. He was well known, his books had sold better than better books, and his portrait had been often in the papers; but that was not the success he had wanted, nor a success that was worth having, and he was honest enough to admit it to himself. The men who really care for their art, who wish above all things to do the best that is in them, do not take the way of the world and the regular salaries of the newspaper offices. They stay outside, reading, writing, painting for themselves, and snatching such golden crumbs as fall within their reach from the tables of publishers, editors, and picture-buyers. They make a living as it were by accident. It is a hard life and a risky: it is deliciously exciting at first, to leap from crag to crag, wherever a slight handhold will preserve you from the abyss, but the time soon comes when you are tired, and wonder, with dulled heart and clouded brain, is it worth while or no? Those who are strong enough to continue are given their own souls to carry in their hands, and those who admit defeat, surrender them, and, knowing in their hearts that they have sold themselves, hide their sorrow in a louder clamour after an easier quest.

The jolliest of the irregulars, in spite of the anxiety of their life, are those who carry on a guerilla warfare for fame and a long struggle for improvement, never having been caught or maimed by the newspaper routine, or by the drudgery of commercial art work. (For artists as well as writers have an easy way to a livelihood, which they also must have strength to resist.) Some men live as free lances, by selling their articles to such papers as are willing to admit their transcendent worth, and ready to pay some small nominal rate, a guinea a thousand words perhaps, for the privilege of printing them. Many live by reviewing, getting half a dozen books a week from different papers, reading or skimming them, and writing as long a paragraph as the editor will allow on each volume. The artists coax dealers into buying small pictures at a cheap rate, satisfying their pride by contemplation of the vastly larger price at which their purchasers seem to value them as soon as they appear in the glamour of the window. Others again, artists and writers too, these perhaps the most sincere and admirable of the lot, refuse any degradation of their art, and live hand to mouth by any sort of work that offers. There was one man who wrote poems in the intervals of stage carpentry, and another who made dolls while compiling a history of philosophy. Some indeed seem able to live on nothing at all, and these are more cheerful than the rest whose stomachs are less accommodating.

There are compensations to poverty, and one of them is extravagance. Goldsmith would not so have enjoyed the pomp of his bloom-coloured suits and his gorgeous Brick Court chambers if he had not known an earlier and different life:

"Where the Red Lion, staring o'er the way,
Invites each passing stranger that can pay;
Where Calvert's butt and Parson's black champagne
Regale the drabs and bloods of Drury Lane;
There in a lonely room, from bailiffs snug,
The Muse found Scroggen stretched beneath a rug;
A window, patched with paper, lent a ray
That dimly showed the state in which he lay;
The sanded floor, that grits beneath the tread;
The humid wall with paltry pictures spread;
The royal game of goose was there in view,
And the twelve rules the Royal Martyr drew;
The Seasons, framed with listing, found a place,
And brave Prince William showed his lamp-black face;
The morn was cold; he views with keen desire
The rusty grate unconscious of a fire:
With beer and milk arrears the frieze was scored,
And five crack'd teacups dress'd the chimney board;
A night-cap decked his brows instead of bay,
A cap by night—a stocking all the day!"

Johnson enjoyed his pension and all that it meant the more for having known a time when he spent the night hours with Richard Savage walking round and round St. James's Square, for want of a lodging, inveighing cheerfully against the Ministry, and "resolving they would stand by their country."

The moments of opulence when they come are the brighter gold for the grey anxiety that has gone before. They make extravagance a joy in itself, and even change the distresses of the past into a charming memory.

I had lived once for over a week on a diet of cheese and apples—cheap yellow cheese and apples at twopence or a penny halfpenny a pound. A friend, also impoverished, was sharing my expenses and my diet, and slept in a small room in the same house. Our two sleeping boxes, for they were no more, were on the ground floor, and a large fat postman, our landlord, slept in the basement underneath. On the Wednesday of the second week, by the three o'clock post, came a letter for my friend, from a literary agent, containing a cheque for twenty-five pounds—TWENTY-FIVE POUNDS! It is an amazing fact, but I do believe the tears came into our eyes at the sight of that little slip of magenta-coloured paper. We shook hands hysterically, and then—remembering that the bank closed at four—unshaved as we were, without collars, with baggy trousers, we took a hansom for the town. The cheque was cashed, and that somehow seemed a marvel, as the five-pound notes and the gold were slid over the counter in a way most astonishingly matter-of-fact. We went out of the bank doors with a new dignity, paid the cabby, and walked the Strand like giants. It became quite a question what place was best worthy of the honour of entertaining us to tea. Wherever it was—I fancy a small café—it did its duty, and we sat, refreshed and smoking (new opened packets of the best tobacco) while we planned our evening.

At half-past six we went up to Soho, and crossed Leicester Square with solemnity, as befitted men with an aim in life, and that so philanthropic as to dine better that night than ever in their lives before. There was no undignified hurry about our walk, but there was no lingering. I was rebuked for glancing at the window of a print shop, and in my turn remonstrated equally gravely with him for dallying over some pretty editions at a bookseller's in Shaftesbury Avenue.

We dined at one of our favourite little restaurants: we dined excellently, drank several bottles of wine, and had liqueur glasses of rum emptied into our coffees. We smoked, paid the bill, and went out into the narrow Soho street. Just opposite, at the other side, where we could not help seeing it as we hesitated on the pavement, was another of our favourite feeding places. The light was merry through the windows, the evening was young, and—without speaking a word, we looked at each other, and looked at each other again, and then, still without speaking, walked across the street, went in at the inviting door, and had dinner over again—an excellent dinner, good wine, and rum in coffee as before.

Remember the week's diet of apples and cheese before you condemn us. We argued it out as we smoked over our second coffees, and convinced ourselves clearly that if our two dinners had been spread evenly and with taste over our last ten most ill-nourished days, we should not yet have had the food that honest men deserve, That being so, we stood upon our rights, and gave clear consciences to our grateful stomachs.

On our way home we met an old acquaintance, whose hospitality a few days before would have been as manna from heaven, but whose port, good though it was, was now almost superfluous. We reached our lodgings at three in the morning, and my last memory of the festival is that of my friend, usually a rather melancholy man, sitting on my bed drumming with his feet upon the floor, and singing Gaelic songs at the top of his voice, to a zealous accompaniment on my penny whistle. From below came a regular grunting monotone—the landlord snoring in bed. Presently there was a deep thud that startled us for a moment into quiet. We listened, and almost at once the snoring boomed again, as the postman slumbered on the floor where he had fallen. Then we continued our minstrelsy.

It is an up-and-down life, my friends—it is indeed.

TALKING, DRINKING, AND SMOKING

(WITH A PROCESSION OF DRINKING SONGS)

TALKING, DRINKING, AND SMOKING

(WITH A PROCESSION OF DRINKING SONGS)

TALKING, drinking, and smoking go better together than any three other pleasant things upon this earth. And they are best enjoyed in company, which is almost as much as to say that they are not best performed at home. Individually they may be;—a pipe over your own fire, a glass of wine close by the elbow of your own easy-chair, a quiet comfortable talk with your particular friend, whose opinions you know before they are uttered, are severally very delightful. But if good liquor, talk, and smoke are to be enjoyed to the utmost, why then, get you half a dozen honest fellows about you, with no particular qualification, and have your evening out. Go to a tavern or a coffee-house, where you will be left to yourselves. Be free from womenfolk, with their pestilential seriousness or more aggravating flippancy. Get you and your company into a cosy room, with a bright fire and a closed door, where you may be free men before the universe. Then may your words express the mood you feel, the liquor hearten you, and the smoke soothe you in argument; and if with that you are not happy, why, then, the devil fly away with you for a puritanical, melancholiac spoilsport, whom I would not see with my book in his hands, no, not for four shillings and sixpence on the nail.

No, sir, if you cannot be happy so, why, you are a fellow unclubable, unsociable, a creature without human instincts—no true man. I'll have none of you, and if your name come up for election at any of our clubs, I'll blackball you with all my heart, and wish the ball were twice as black and twice as big.

Not that I am a friend to drunkenness and bestiality: far from it. Only children lick honey from the spoon. But spread honey with bread and butter, and season good liquor with mirth and company, talk and tobacco, and either is a gift from the gods. Nor do tavern crawls, those itinerant extravagances, stand higher in my favour, dear though they are to the irregulars who practise them. To sup with ale at the Cheshire Cheese, to drink at the Punch Bowl, at the Green Dragon, at the Mitre, at the Cock, at the Grecian, at the George, at the Edinburgh—in short, to beat the bounds of every tavern in Fleet Street, from Ludgate Circus to the Strand, that is a festival too peripatetic to be comfortable, an undertaking too serious to be light-hearted.

But you, sir, who smile at the thought of beer—or is it port or sherry, or perhaps good, rollicking, stout-flavoured rum ?—who dream joyfully of brown-walled rooms, of tables worn and polished, covered with stained rings where the bounty of innumerable glasses has over-flowed their brims, whose eyes are alight with the fire of the fine things you are ready to say, whose pipe is even now in your hands, you are a man of another sort and the right one. You do not forget that the first and proudest of man's inventions when his reason came to him was a club, that Bacchus was the favourite of the ancient gods, and Silenus the most lovable of the sub-divinities. You remember that the Scandinavian heaven was a club, Valhalla, where the heroes met to enjoy themselves, and fight with swords even as we fight with arguments, and after the fighting to

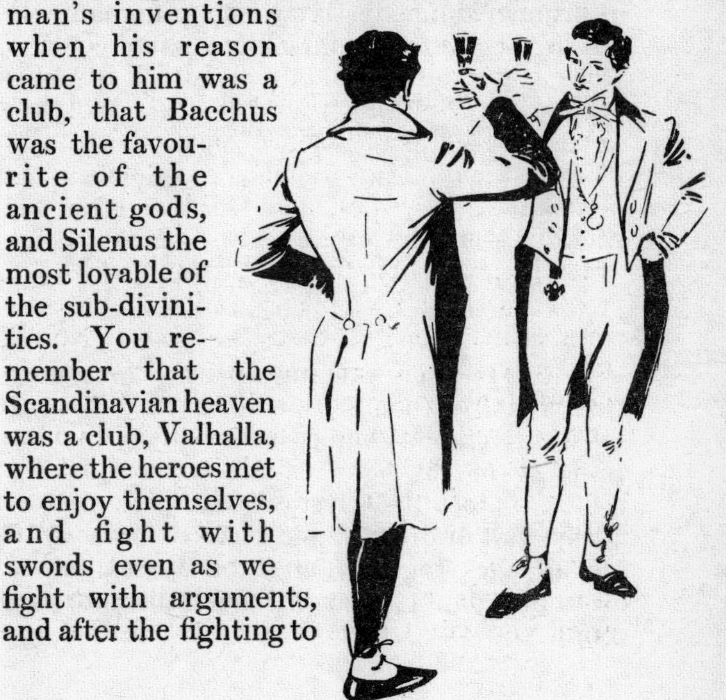

drink, and sing, and be good fellows one to the other. You regret each century for the merry companionable evenings you have missed by living in another time. You, and you alone, will read with the right understanding, with a smile of sympathetic memory, with no lemon-juiced condemnation tightening your lips.

What an illustrious company is ours: Ben Jonson, Beaumont, Fletcher, Herrick, Congreve—the list would fill the book. Cromwell was not against us, and even Doctor Johnson (although he did drink port, bottle by bottle, in his own company—a swinish, inhuman procedure) wrote for us our philosophy:

> "Hermit hoar in solemn cell,
> Wearing out life's evening gray,
> Strike thy bosom sage, and tell,
> What is bliss, and which the way?
>
> Thus I spoke, and speaking sighed,
> Scarce repressed the starting tear,
> When the hoary sage replied,
> 'Come, my lad, and drink some beer.'"

Once, after an evening spent in a tavern with a mob of honest, open-hearted fellows, I sat in my chair at home, before going to bed, thinking of the older time. I was smoking the last pipe, the mystical last pipe that is always full of dreams, and seemed suddenly to see all ages together, and the Bohemians of all time coming through the walls into my room,

Ben Jonson, pimple-nosed, strong-headed, appeared sitting in an easy-chair, as if in the Devil room at the Apollo, reading a paper sent him from his friend Master Beaumont, who was busy with Master Fletcher in the country, writing a play. He read aloud:

"Methinks the little wit I had is lost
Since I saw you;"
(honest fellow, Master Beaumont, generous mind!)
"for wit is like a rest
Held up at tennis, which men do the best
With the best gamesters. What things have we seen
Done at the *Mermaid!* heard words that have been
So nimble and so full of subtle flame,
As if that every one from whence they came
Had meant to put his whole wit in a jest,
And had resolved to live a fool the rest
Of his dull life; there where there hath been thrown
Wit able enough to justify the town
For three days past: wit that might warrant be
For the whole city to talk foolishly,
Till that were cancelled; and when that was gone,
We left an air behind us, which alone
Was able to make the next two companies
Right witty; though but downright fools, more wise."

"Aha, they know their Ben. They know him." He fell to murmuring over his own verses:

"Welcome all who lead or follow
To the Oracle of Apollo——
Here he speaks out of his pottle,
Or the tripos, his tower bottle:
All his answers are divine,
Truth itself doth flow in wine.
Hang up all the poor hop-drinkers
Cries old Sim, the king of skinkers;

He the half of life abuses
That sits watering with the Muses.
Those dull girls no good can mean us;
Wine it is the milk of Venus,
And the poet's horse accounted;
Ply it, and you all are mounted.
Tis the true Phœbian liquor,
Cheers the brain, makes wit the quicker;
Pays all debts, cures all diseases,
And at once three senses pleases.
Welcome all who lead or follow
To the Oracle of Apollo."

"A very charming rhyme in praise of grape liquor," I was about to say, "but a little too scornful of ale. Ale is a good drink, and hearty, the parent of as much good prose as ever Spanish wine made good verse." I was about to say this, when I saw a gaily dressed little man, with a tankard in one hand and a sheaf of paper in the other, come walking through my bookcase. I knew Mr. Gay at once, and guessed that he had come to battle for the best of drinks. But, before he could speak, a pretty little parson fellow skipped into the room, bowed unctuously to Ben, shot this verse at him, and withdrew:

"Ah, Ben,
Say how or when
Shall we thy guests
Meet at those lyric feasts,
Made at the *Sun*,
The *Dog*, the *Triple Tun*?
Where we such clusters had
As made us nobly wild, not mad;
And yet each verse of thine
Outdid the meat, outdid the frolic wine."

"Herrick!" cried Ben joyfully, but he was gone, and little Mr. Gay was bowing in his place. Placing his dripping tankard on a new volume of poems that lay on my table, he bowed respectfully to my distinguished guest, and then, laying his left hand easily upon his sword-hilt, sang merrily and with a provocative, mischievous air:

"Whilst some in epic strains delight,
Whilst others pastorals invite,
As taste or whim prevail:
Assist me, all ye tuneful Nine;
Support me in the great design,
To sing of nappy ale.

Some folks of cyder make a rout,
And cyder's well enough no doubt,
When better liquors fail;
But wine, that's richer, better still,
Ev'n wine itself (deny 't who will),
Must yield to nappy ale.

Rum, brandy, gin with choicest smack
From Holland brought, Batavia arrack,
All these will nought avail
To chear a truly British heart,
And lively spirits to impart,
Like humming, nappy ale.

Oh! whether I thee closely hug
In honest can or nut-brown jug,
Or in the tankard hail;
In barrel, or in bottle pent,
I give the generous spirit vent,
Still may I feast on ale.

But chief when to the chearful glass
From vessel pure thy streamlets pass,
  Then most thy charms prevail;
Then, then, I'll bet, and take the odds
That nectar, drink of heathen gods,
  Was poor compar'd to ale.

Give me a bumper, fill it up.
See how it sparkles in the cup,
  Oh, how shall I regale!
Can any taste this drink divine
And then compare rum, brandy, wine,
  Or ought with nappy ale?"

He paused for a moment to take a long drink from the tankard, which he replaced on the poetry book. Then, delicately wiping his lips, which were curved with satisfaction, he went on:

"Inspir'd by thee, the warrior fights,
The lover wooes, the poet writes,
  And pens the pleasing tale;
And still in Britain's isle confess'd
Nought animates the patriot's breast
  Like generous, nappy ale.

High Church and Low oft raise a strife
  And oft endanger limb and life,
Each studious to prevail;
  Yet Whig and Tory, opposite
  In all things else, do both unite
    In praise of nappy ale.

O blest potation! still by thee,
And thy companion Liberty,
  Do health and mirth prevail;
Then let us crown the can, the glass,
And sportive bid the minutes pass
  In quaffing nappy ale.

Ev'n while these stanzas I indite,
The bar bell's grateful sounds invite
 Where joy can never fail!
Adieu! my Muse, adieu! I haste
To gratify my longing taste
 With copious draughts of ALE."

He had scarcely finished, and was emptying the tankard, when John Keats appeared (I had not seen him coming).

"Shades of poets dead and gone,"

he chanted, coughing painfully, but keeping a smiling face, that made kind old Ben Jonson wince:

"Shades of poets dead and gone,
What elysium have ye known,
Happy field or mossy cavern,
Choicer than the Mermaid Tavern?"

"Aha! You are a friend for me, sir!" cried Gay, and taking him familiarly by the arm, walked off with him through the writing desk. They were not ten yards away before they were walking apart, quarrelling vigorously, which was puzzling, till I remembered that Keats was no drinker of nappy ale, but so passionate a lover of wine that he once covered

all the inside of his mouth and throat with cayenne pepper, in order to enjoy "the delicious coolness of claret in all its glory."

"Who is that young man?" asked Ben, but before I could answer him there was the stump, stumping of a wooden leg, and little William Davies stood before us. He was laughing merrily, and sang:

> "Oh, what a merry world I see
> Before me through a quart of ale.
> Now if sometimes that men would laugh,
> And women too would sigh and wail——
> To laugh or wail's an easy task
> For all who drink at my ale-cask." *

"Ale, all ale," interrupted Ben Jonson. "Why do they sing of ale?"

"Here's whisky for you then," cried Davies, and sang mournfully:

> "Whisky, thou blessed heaven in the brain,
> Oh, that the belly should revolt,
> To make a hell of after pain,
> And prove thy virtue was a fault!
>
> Did ever poet seek his bed
> With a sweet phrase upon his lips
> Smiling—as I laid down my head,
> Pleased after sundry whisky-sips?
>
> I pitied all the world: alas!
> That no poor nobodies came near,
> To give to them my shirt and shoes,
> And bid them be of goodly cheer.

A blessed heaven was in the brain;
  But ere came morn the belly turned
And kicked up hell's delight in pain—
  This tongue went dry, this throat it burned.

Oh dear! oh dear! to think last night
  The merriest man on earth was I,
And that I should awake this morn,
  To cough and groan, to heave and sigh!" *

"Nay, nay," said Ben, surprised, "I know nothing of all that."

* * * * *

There are some, who do not understand true enjoyment, will tell you that rules spoil convivial meetings, and that a merry company becomes a dull committee as soon as it is called a club. Do not believe them: the precedents are all against them. Unless you have a club to regulate the times and seasons of your mirth you are likely enough to be merry when your friends are sad, and melancholy when they are joyful. Whereas, if all the week you have a pleasant consciousness that on Wednesday, say, or Thursday night there will be jollity, you go to the tavern in the proper spirit, and smile before you turn the door. And as for rules, why, rules are half the fun. You remember Ben Jonson's own:

* From "New Poems." By William Davies. Published by Mr. Elkin Mathews.

Idiota, insulsus, tristis, turpis, abesto.
Eruditi, urbani, hilares, honesti, adsciscuntor;
Nec lectæ feminæ repudiantor.
De discubitu non contenditor.
Vina puris fontibus ministrantor aut vapulet hospes.
Insipida poemata nulla recitantor.
Amatoriis querelis, ac suspiriis liber angulus esto.
Qui foras vel dicta, vel facta eliminet, eliminator.

There are some of them, and are they not admirably contrived? (Though I suspect the third, and the one about a corner for lovers were dictated by some momentary caprice of the poet himself, contrary as they are to all the best practice in England. In France it has always been the thing: the student's mistress hears her lord discuss; but here, until very lately, men have talked and smoked to themselves.) The neat compliment to the members insinuated by the first and second—no objectionables admitted, and the whole company able to congratulate themselves as learned, urbane, jolly, and honest men—is delightful. There was to be no squabbling for places; the wine was to be kept at a good level of quality by the simplest means; no fool to interrupt the flow of talk with his tasteless verse, and all reporters to be expelled. What evenings those must have been. It is easy to imagine the door open to each new-comer primed up with hope of happiness, glancing about to see which of his friends were there before him, and bowing to receive a nod from the great Ben. And late at night, when all was over, can you not envy them, strolling,

rolling, tumbling, strutting out into the moonlight of old Temple Bar, with their heads full of wholesome wit and wine?

Then, for another set of rules, remember those "enacted by a Knot of Artizans and Mechanics," as Addison read them "upon the wall in a little Alehouse."

"I. Every Member at his first coming shall lay down his Two Pence.

"II. Every Member shall fill his Pipe out of his own Box.

"III. If any Member absents himself he shall forfeit a Penny for the Use of the Club, unless in Case of Sickness or Imprisonment.

"IV. If any Member swears or curses, his Neighbour may give him a Kick upon the Shins.

"V. If any Member tells Stories in the Club that are not true, he shall forfeit for every third Lie a Halfpenny.

"VI. If any Member strikes another wrongfully, he shall pay his Club for him.

"VII. If any Member brings his Wife into the Club, he shall pay for whatever she drinks or smoaks.

"VIII. If any Member's wife comes to fetch him home from the Club, she shall speak to him without the Door.

"IX. If any Member calls another Cuckold, he shall be turned out of the Club.

"X. None shall be admitted into the Club

that is of the same Trade with any Member of it.

"XI. None of the Club shall have his Clothes or Shoes made or mended but by a Brother Member.

"XII. No Non-juror shall be capable of being a Member."

The humorous third rule, the somewhat disconcerting fifth, the cynical eighth, all these are pleasant, but the tenth and twelfth contain more club wisdom than all the others put together. For the tenth rule secures to each member the right to speak on one subject with authority. Silenced, for example, in an argument on knife-grinding, the carpenter can solace himself by bragging of his exclusive knowledge of joinery, a solid comfort that would vanish if a rival carpenter should cross the threshold—for then, at the moment of the poor fellow's discomfiture, when still weak from the conflict with the grinder of knives, his supremacy in his own business might be usurped, and he be left nincompoop for ever. And as for the twelfth rule, it is the neatest conceived of safeguards against faddists. It is as if we in one of our clubs were to prohibit vegetarians or anti-vaccinationists. It is a charming testimony to the beef and beer sanity of the members (a shoemaker and a tailor from internal evidence.—— How ingratiating looks "Brother Member" on the paper!) who wrote the rules.

It is impossible to get away from the rules of the old clubs before listening for a moment to those that governed "the moral philosophers, as they called themselves, who assembled twice a week, in order to show the absurdity of the present mode of religion and establish a new one in its stead." Their rules, as Goldsmith says, "will give a most just idea of their learning and principles." Some of his own clubs cannot have been very different.

"I. We being a laudable society of moral philosophers, intends to dispute twice a week about religion and priestcraft; leaving behind us old wives' tales, and following good learning and sound sense: and if so be that any other persons has a mind to be of the society, they shall be entitled so to do, upon paying the sum of three shillings, to be spent by the company in punch.

"II. That no member get drunk before nine of the clock, upon pain of forfeiting three pence, to be spent by the company in punch.

"III. That, as members are sometimes apt to go way without paying, every person shall pay sixpence upon his entering the room; and all disputes shall be settled by a majority, and all fines shall be paid in punch.

"IV. That sixpence shall be every night given to the president, in order to buy books of learning for the good of the society: the president has already put himself to a good deal of expense in buying books for the club;

particularly the works of Tully, Socrates, and Cicero, which he will soon read to the society.

V. All them who brings a new argument against religion, and who being a philosopher and a man of learning, as the rest of us is, shall be admitted to the freedom of the society, upon paying sixpence only, to be spent in punch.

VI. Whenever we are to have an extraordinary meeting, it shall be advertised by some outlandish name in the newspapers.

SANDERS MACWILD, *President.*
ANTHONY BLEWIT, *Vice-President,*
his X mark.
WILLIAM TURPIN, *Secretary.*

* * * * *

What clubs there must have been; and yet why regret them? What clubs there are to-day; what clubs there will be until man changes his nature, and becomes an animal that does not talk, or drink, or smoke. If you, O honest, not inhuman, reader, ever find your way into Bohemia, my best wish for you is a club, a company of fellows as jolly as yourself, a good cosy room, a free-burning hearth, plenty of whatever tobacco smokes best in your pipe, of whatever liquor flows easiest in your gullet, of whatever talk, of poetry, of romance, of pictures, sounds sweetest in your ears. Or, if you have been in Bohemia, and now are far away, or grown old, may this chapter suggest the evenings of your youth, and (but it would need to be better written) bring back something of the old good fellowship that made those evenings so hearty a delight.

OLD AND NEW HAMPSTEAD

OLD AND NEW HAMPSTEAD

It is only lately that Hampstead has become an integral part of London; only a century since one could be stopped by highwaymen on one's way into town from the Heath. It used to be the most beautiful country within reach of the city, and so a proper place for "shoemakers' holidays" and for retirement. Even now you may go to sleep behind a bush in one of the little wooded valleys of the Heath, and doubt on waking if you are not in a dream, when you hear the bells of London churches strike the hours. In those older days, when there were fewer houses, and the city had not yet swept the edge of the green with her dusty grey petticoat, it was no wonder that Hampstead was loved by men of letters chained to the neighbourhood of the town.

Steele's cottage was on Haverstock Hill, just opposite "The Load of Hay," and within easy walking distance of "The Upper Flask," "The Bull and Bush," "The Spaniards," and the other taverns of the Heath. Here he came to work, but doubtless often found that "the sun was on the other side of the road," and stepped over to "The Load of Hay." Or perhaps he made the pot-boy of the inn carry the sunlight over to him in a pewter tankard. Here he lived, like the untidy, pleasant creature that he was, half gentleman and Captain of the Guards, half just jolly humanity, the friend of all the world. He was more often Dick than Captain Steele.

Up Haverstock Hill on summer days came as many of the "thirty-nine noblemen and gentlemen, zealously attached to the Protestant succession of the House of Hanover," as thought it worth their while to journey out from town to the meetings of the Kit Cat Club at "The Upper Flask." There would be Addison, sure to call for the better half of the *Spectator* on the way. Or if not Addison, then another of them would find Steele, doubtless pretending to be busy, but really waiting eagerly for the call that would persuade him from his labours. Then, at "The Upper Flask," they would drink, and perhaps sing, and certainly talk, as they sat under a mulberry tree enjoying the fresh air and each other's society.

"The Spaniards" inn too has its history. Goldsmith met there with his less reputable friends, the friends with whom he could "rattle away carelessly," without dread of Doctor Johnson's conversational bludgeon. And in later times it shared with "Jack Straw's Castle" the affections of Dickens, who gave Mrs. Bardell an afternoon there with her friends, the afternoon that was so cruelly interrupted by the terrors of the law. Dickens wrote to Forster in 1837 : " You don't feel disposed, do you, to muffle yourself up, and start off with me for a good brisk walk over Hampstead Heath? I knows a good 'ouse there where we can have a red-hot chop for dinner, and a glass of good wine." It is easy to picture them at it, and the taste for red-hot chops continues still, and often in the summer twos and threes go up to walk the Heath and feed at one or other of its inns, and still there are clubs that meet to chatter at " The Spaniards " or " The Bull and Bush."

Lamb knew the Heath; sorrowfully upon occasion, when he walked hand in hand with his sister, taking her to the asylum at Finchley when her old mania showed any sign of an outbreak; merrily enough though at Leigh Hunt's, and quite pleasantly by himself:

" I do not remember a more whimsical surprise than having been once detected—by a familiar damsel—reclined at my ease upon the grass, on Primrose Hill (her Cythera) reading 'Pamela.' There was nothing in the book to make a man seriously ashamed at the exposure; but as she seated herself down by me, and seemed determined to read in company, I could have wished it had been—any other book. We read on very sociably for a few pages; and, not finding the author much to her taste, she got up, and—went away. Gentle casuist, I leave it to thee to conjecture, whether the blush (for there was one between us) was the property of the nymph or the swain in this dilemma. From me you shall never get the secret."

Leigh Hunt had "a little packing-case of a cottage" in the Vale of Health. There never was such a man for illustrating his own character. When he was in prison he decorated his room with painted roses; and see how he shows his pride in the very cottaginess of his cottage. "I defy you," says he, "to have lived in a smaller cottage than I have done. Yet," he continues, "it has held Shelley, and Keats, and half a dozen friends in it at once." There is a good deal of Leigh Hunt in those two sentences. He loved to retire there to work, out of the bustle of London; and there were spent the evenings that Shelley remembered in Italy, in the little room that Keats describes:

> ". . . . . the chimes
> Of friendly voices had just given place
> To as sweet a silence, when I 'gan retrace
> The pleasant day, upon a couch at ease.
> It was a poet's house who keeps the keys
> Of pleasure's temple. Round about were hung
> The glorious features of the bards who sung
> In other ages—cold and sacred busts
> Smiled at each other . . . . .
> . . . .
>
> Sappho's meek head was there half smiling down
> At nothing; just as though the earnest frown

Of over thinking had that moment gone
From off her brow, and left her all alone.

Great Alfred's, too, with anxious pitying eyes,
As if he always listened to the sighs
Of the goaded world; and Kosciusko's worn
By horrid suff'rance—mightily forlorn.

Petrarch, outstepping from the shady green,
Starts at the sight of Laura; nor can wean
His eyes from her sweet face. Most happy they!
For over them was seen a fair display
Of outspread wings, and from between them shone
The face of Poesy: from off her throne
She overlook'd things that I scarce could tell.
The very sense of where I was might well
Keep Sleep aloof: but more than that, there came
Thought after thought to nourish up the flame
Within my breast; so that the morning light
Surprised me even from a sleepless night;
And up I rose refresh'd, and glad, and gay,
Resolving to begin that very day
These lines; and howsoever they be done,
I leave them as a father does his son."

Hazlitt came here to listen to Leigh Hunt "running on and talking about himself at his own fireside." Hazlitt thought Hunt a "delightful coxcomb," and doubtless told him so. "Mr. Hunt ought to have been a gentleman born, and to have patronised men of letters. He might then have played, and sung, and laughed, and talked his life away."

All that set of men loved the Heath. Leigh Hunt found it an admirable place for studying Italian landscapes; Shelley used to run about it in the dark, leaping over the bushes, and shouting like an exuberant imp let out in upper air. Coleridge finished his life out at Highgate, on the other side; and Keats bought the Heath for himself by right of song. Here he wrote the "Ode to a Nightingale," and he lived at one time in Well Walk, lodging with a postman, and at another in John Street, where he was next door to Fanny Brawne. From the time of the Kit Cats the place has never been without its writers; and as for painters—Romney, Collins, Linnell, Constable, Madox Brown, Kate Greenaway: need the list be continued further?

To-day things are different. Hampstead is no longer a fashionable watering-place some way out of London; it is within half an hour of the middle of the town. It has suffered from its own reputation, and become a stronghold of the "literary life," which is a very different thing from the honest, hardworking existence of men like Hunt or Keats. It is the home of people who have had trivial successes, and live on in the sequestered happiness of forgotten celebrities, and of the people who have been able to spend their lives playing amiably at art or literature. Painters who can no longer paint, poets whose fame has penetrated the suburban wildernesses and become no more than notoriety, journalists who have never had their day, all live here together, a curious unreal life like fragile puppets in a toy theatre. The place has the feeling of a halfway house between this world and the next.

Its convention of unconventionality is too

rigid for Bohemia. Every one is congratulating every one on being so different from every one else. No one is content to live as life has made them and as they are. Indeed, there would be no chapter about the place in this book if it were not that young writers and painters so often get their first queer foretaste of reputation in the Hampstead salons. For there is competition among the wives of the elderly critics and the elderly minor poets, who wish to make their houses centres of intellectual life, to collect the most youthful specimens of genius, and to hear, as from the mouths of babes and sucklings, the meanings and messages of "the newer movements." A dozen charming middle-aged women struggle, with the aid of Messrs. Liberty and a painful expenditure of taste, to turn their drawing-rooms into salons. And a young man cannot be long in the life of the studios or the reviews without being introduced to one of them.

Ah, the Hampstead salon. Imagine a room papered in delicate green, with white mouldings dividing the walls and white paint along the cornices, and a fringe of Hobbema trees running round below the ceiling. The room has half a dozen nooks and corners, and in each corner, seated on cushions, are a young man with long hair and flowing tie, and a maiden out of a Burne-Jones picture, reading poetry, listening to the talk or to the music made by a youthful Paderewski at the piano. The hostess will be draped in green or brown, to tone with the wall-papers, and she will talk anxiously with one or another young man, thinking all the time about the intellectual level of the conversation and the balance of her sentences. And the talk? In the corners of the room it will be of poetry, or ideals in art or politics; but through all will run a deeper, more serious note. Some cause, some movement, some great and vital matter will stir the whole salon. For Hampstead has always her causes, forsaken one by one as some new Pied Piper carries the ladies after him. A man will address the hostess and shake his fist, and talk of Ireland, and the brutality of English rule; of the deplorable condition of the Russian peasants; of the open shame of the Ipecacuanha Indians, who prefer tattoo to decent clothing. "Shall these things be?" he asks. "What, tell me, is to become of liberty, of humanity, of civilisation, if Hampstead pass by on the other side of the way?" What indeed? Several committees will be formed at once.

I have a tenderness for the people in the corners; with them lies hope. It is not their fault if they have been brought up in the masquerade; nor are they much to blame if they have mistaken its doors (with imitation old English latches) for the gates of the promised land where convention is no more, and art and poetry flourish together like birds in the dawn. A salmon-coloured tie may really help a young poet to be himself; it only becomes abhorrent when it is put on as a fashionable affectation. Long and matted hair is quite intelligibly worn by the young men who are mad to "return to the primitive emotions of healthy barbaric life" (I quote from a Hampstead conversation). It is certainly entertaining to watch the chase of barbaric emotion in a Hampstead drawing-room—but we can be grateful for amusement. And if we ask for seriousness of purpose—it was one of these Hampstead poets who wrote on his birthday: "Eighteen to-day . . . And NOTHING done!" You cannot have anything much more serious than that.

A WEDDING IN BOHEMIA

A WEDDING IN BOHEMIA

A SCULPTOR and a painter girl fell in love with each other, and, as they had neither money nor prospect of getting any, had nothing to wait for, and so got married at once. A cousin of the sculptor, not knowing what was on foot, unexpectedly ordered a bust, and paid him twenty pounds: with so much opulence, they decided to spend their honeymoon in the Latin Quarter.

We were very fond of them both, and held a consultation on the matter. Was it right, was it fitting, we asked, that these two should be married and have no wedding party? Let us uphold the honour of the arts, and give them a send off. Things were very well with some of us, and we were sure of a couple of sovereigns, so four of us set off through the back streets of Bloomsbury to a small French restaurant that had always held us welcome.

"A wedding party?" asked madame of the restaurant. "And who of you is to be married? Monsieur the sculptor—quel brave garçon—and the mademoiselle si petite, si jolie." She was delighted, and promised us the upstairs room to ourselves, and said she would do her best for us. We separated, to whip up the guests, collect the money, buy some roses in Covent Garden, and borrow a famous and gigantic loving-cup that has taken its part in a dozen celebrations. We bought a modelling tool and a huge cheap paintbrush, and decorated them with ribbons.

Our party met that evening at the Mad Club, twelve men and women, determined on enjoyment. The sculptor, who had shaved his beard for the blessed occasion, arrived last, with the little painter girl. He was twenty-two, and she nineteen, and we greeted them with cheers. Then, delighting in the envy of the rest of the Club, who had not been invited, and had the bad taste to laugh at our enthusiasm, we set off in procession. A sturdy fellow with an accordion, which he had promised not to play in the streets, marched in front, side by side with our principal poet, who had composed a wedding ode. Then came the bride and bridegroom; then three girls, two students, and a model, with their attendant men; and lastly a big fat Scotch writer of humorous stories, and me with a penny whistle. Our satisfaction with ourselves was sublime, and showed itself, in spite of the prohibition, in spasms of melody on the way. We walked merrily, shouting jokes from rank to rank, up Long Acre, across Holborn, and then to the right from Southampton Row, until we reached the restaurant.

When we turned the last corner, we saw, far away at the other end of the grey street, the black and white figure of a waiter standing expectant in the middle of the road. At the sight of our procession he hurriedly disappeared, and when we reached the door madame in person, big, red-cheeked, blue-bloused, white-aproned, was standing smiling on the threshold.

The sculptor turned timorously to the rear ranks: "She does not know which of us it is?" he whispered, with fear in his voice. But she enlightened him herself.

"Ah, Monsieur et Madame," she cried, breaking into the midst of us, and seizing the hands of the bride and bridegroom. "You have the best of my wishes for the happy married life, the dear love, and the large family. Your little wife, is she not so charming, so beautiful? . . . . Your husband, ce bon garçon, is he not so well-set-up? All is ready," she laughed a welcome to the rest of us: "the wine has come,

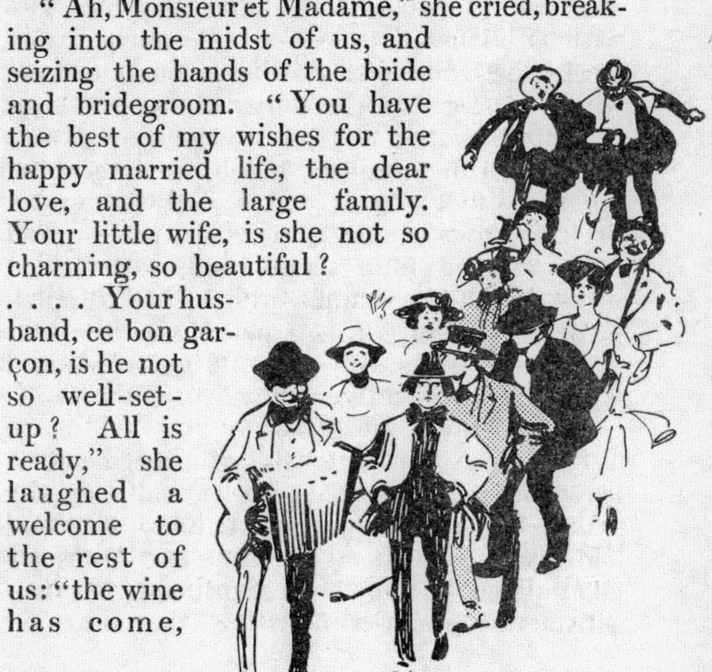

and the bouillon is hot; it is Monsieur's favourite bouillon," she added, turning again to the sculptor, "and for Madame I have made a salade with my own hands. . . . Ah, the happy married life, Monsieur et Madame."

Upstairs madame had kept her promises. Bottles ranged down the table, and the red and white roses made a rare show. A paper crown, looked upon lovingly by the Frenchwoman as her own work, folded and frizzed like the decoration to a tart, lay on the plate of the bride, and a huge cigar, a present from madame's husband, lay on the plate of the bridegroom. The paint brush and the modelling tool, gay with ribbons, lay crossed between them. Corks flew from bottles with a joyous crackling. Madame stood in the doorway, her hands on her hips, shouting joyfully to the waiter to be quick with the bouillon, which presently came up in a vast tureen. She sent the waiter packing down again, to bring up her shy red husband, made him shake hands with the lot of us, and then remained after he had escaped, to hear the sculptor, in a nervous, efflorescent speech, acknowledge the gifts of crown and cigar and the effective symbolism of the paint-brush and the moulder.

Indeed, she could not find it in her heart to leave us. She waited on us, bullying the waiter out of the jollity of her heart, and addressing remarks all the time to "Monsieur et Madame," a huge smile expressing her own satisfaction, and a crimson face the confusion of the little painter girl, while the sculptor pretended not to mind. The soup was served, and the waiter vanished regretfully, as the rest of the meal was to be cold, and we had agreed to help ourselves . . . Surely she was going. No. "Pardon, Monsieur et Madame," she beamed in the faces of the uncomfortable two, and rearranged their knives and forks. Again she tried to go, again was overcome by the fascination of the newly married. "Que je suis imbécile,"—she shuffled back and altered the position of the flowers in the middle of the table. "Oh, Monsieur et Madame," she murmured, smiling with as matronly an enjoyment as if the pretty little painter had been one of her own stout daughters. Suddenly the sculptor's self-possession left him. He put down his spoon, and fairly loosed himself in laughter, and the good woman, enjoying but not in the least understanding the joke, threw her head back and laughed uproariously with him. Some one lifted the loving-cup. "Yes, yes!" we shouted. "To the health of Monsieur et Madame!" "To Monsieur et Madame!" she said with fervour, and holding the great bowl between her fat jewelled hands, she drank. How we laughed. She set the loving-cup on the table, and, suddenly bending over, kissed the little bride on the forehead. How we cheered. Then at last she went out. "Oh, Monsieur et Madame," we heard her gurgle as she closed the door.

That set the dinner going gaily. The food

disappeared, and the beer, and the wine. We made speeches ; we sang ; the poet recited his ode ; we made the little bride put on her paper crown, and compelled her husband to smoke his gigantic cigar ; the loving-cup passed round twice, and then could go round no more except as the emblem of a vanished joy. There was a piano in a corner of the room, and when we left the table we did a little dancing ; the man with the accordion used it well, the penny whistle sounded, and one of the bridesmaids, who was an art student, sat at the piano with a painter, to play a ten-finger duet, their spare hands clasped about each other's waists. At half-past ten we begin to be thirsty again with our merriment, and there was no wine or indeed drink of any kind in the place, for the restaurant had no licence. The street door had been shut a quarter of an hour before. We had to draw lots as to who should go out to replenish the canteen. Two were to go—the one to see, as somebody impertinently suggested, that none of the precious liquor was drunk upon the way—and the lot fell on the fat story-writer and me. The others were to let us in from the street, as soon as they heard us knock.

Ideals cause a great deal of discomfort. There was really no need for us to have any ; we could have been contented with wine—but our ideal was crème de menthe. In other parts of the town you have but to ask for crème de menthe to see it handed over the counter ; but here it was a different matter. We got our dozen of cheap bad claret with ease, and borrowed a basket to carry it in ; but we went to at least eight little shops in those back streets before we found a man who had ever heard of the liqueur. At last we found a spirit-shop with a very intelligent proprietor, whose intelligence we welcomed, that afterwards we had cause to curse.

"Crème de menthe," he said ; "is not that the same as essence of peppermint?"

"Yes, surely." We had heard something of the sort. "Anyhow, it is always sold in narrow bottles."

The man went downstairs behind the counter, and we heard him strike a match and move about in the cellar under our feet. Presently he came up with two very big bottles.

"At least these are the right shape."

We bought them, and, laden with our purchases, set off eagerly back to the restaurant.

All the lights were out below stairs, and the blinds were down in the windows of the room our party were enjoying. The accordion was going merrily, and several voices were singing different songs. We banged and thundered on the door, but they were making too much noise for anybody in the house to hear us. Standing well back from the pavement, I began to throw pennies at the lighted windows. The first penny touched the cornice, fell in the gutter, and rolled away irretrievably in the darkness of the street. The second hit the sill, and dropped through the grating into the basement. The third, the fourth followed its example. There was no other missile left but my latch-key. The other fellow had nothing at all.

"You'll have to make a good shot, and smash the window, or else you'll lose the key. We'll make those deaf idiots share the expense."

I took a step back, and a deliberate aim, and then let fly. There was a crash of falling glass as the latch-key fell inside the room. The music stopped, the blind was pulled aside, and half a dozen of the rogues trooped downstairs, let us in with cheerful apologies, and took the claret bottles from the basket as we carried it up.

The crème de menthe, the prize of the evening, was to be kept to the end, and we gave ourselves up gladly to singing, and drinking the claret. It had been found that the poet's rather solemn epithalamium fitted admirably to a popular music-hall tune; it was rendered with energy, and such success that even the poet, inclined to be unhappy at first, at last joined in good-temperedly, and sang as loudly as the rest. It was very late when we took the first of those long bottles, opened it with elaborate ostentation, and poured a green liquid into the empty wineglasses. Thank goodness, it was the right colour.

"Health!" cried the sculptor, "to the two brave fellows who gave their all (for did they not leave us, and is not merriment such as ours the sum of human joy) to bring us this liqueur. Gentlemen, brother artists, your very good health!"

The glasses, shimmering with dark green, were lifted, and ten happy men and women drank to our prosperity. I have seldom seen ten faces flash with such perfect unanimity from exultation to dismay. Their mouths screwed up. Their eyes blinked. They put the glasses unsteadily down.

"You two fellows had better drink our healths now," was the sculptor's only comment, as he set his glass on the mantelpiece, with the tears in his eyes, and wrinkles round his mouth as if he had been drinking lemon juice.

We sipped gingerly, walked to the window, and hurled the bottles that had cost so much to sudden chaos on the opposite pavement. So much for ideals.

Just then the big French lady opened the door. "It is half-past twelve," she said; "I regret much that you must go." She looked round the room for the bride, and smiled again her prodigious wonderful smile. "The bill? Ah yes. That is quite right."

"We have broken a window," said the sculptor. He had insisted that the window at least should be paid for by himself.

Madame smiled again. "Ah oui. A window. It is the youth. One does not get married every day. The window shall be my wedding gift to Monsieur et Madame." She caught the young sculptor, who had unwarily approached too near, and kissed him loudly on either cheek. I am really happy to record the fact—he kissed her in return.

And so the twelve of us bundled out into the street again, half-an-hour after midnight, leaving madame waving farewells from the door. This time we did not walk in twos and twos. Our hearts were high, and needed a more general comradeship. We walked twelve deep, arm in arm, along the narrow streets, to the tune, or something like the tune, of the "Soldiers' Chorus," played bravely on the accordion. It was not genteel; it was perhaps a little vulgar; but it was tremendously genuine.

We went to a flat in the Gray's Inn Road that was rented by two of the men. As long as the wine and the jollity kept us awake we made speeches, and sang, and prophesied of the success of the sculptor, and told stories without point that seemed prodigious witty. Gradually we grew sleepier and sleepier, and at last were all asleep, some on the divans, some in chairs, some on the floor with heads on cushions or backs propped against the wall. . . . We awoke only just in time to take the two children, bride and bridegroom, to the station, where their luggage, such as it was, was waiting for them, and to see them off, dishevelled, dirty, weary as ourselves, in the morning boat train for Paris.

A NOVELIST

A NOVELIST

It is a joyous day for a young man when one of his articles wins him a letter from a well-known writer. I walked through Bloomsbury with elation, feeling, square in my pocket, the note that invited me to call on a novelist whose work had given me a paragraph in one of my diminutive essays. He was so well known that it was a little surprising to find him in Bloomsbury at all. Why not in St. John's Wood? I asked. Why not in the real country? At least I pictured a very sumptuous flat. Through the old streets I walked, through the squares of tall old houses once fashionable but now infested by landladies, expecting all the time, as I neared the street he had mentioned, to find more signs of opulence. I found it at last, and it was dingy, miserable, more depressing than the rest. The novelist lived at number seven. I rang the bell and waited with a fluttering heart.

Presently the door opened a suspicious six inches, and the tousled head of an elderly woman in curl-papers showed itself in the opening. On asking for my novelist, I was told to come in, and driven into the usual lodging-house dining-room. A huge gilt mirror hung over the mantelpiece, faded rhododendrons upside down made a grisly pattern on the wall-paper, the table was covered with a purple tasselled cloth with holes in it, and the furniture was upholstered in a material that had once been pink. The curtains drawn across the windows were yellow and grey with age and dust, and I could not bear to look at the carpet. There were four pictures on the walls, portraits of Queen Victoria and Mr. Gladstone, and two enlarged photographs, coloured, and magnificently framed, that showed the curl-papered lady who had opened the door, dressed in a low-necked evening gown, with jewels about her fat creased neck, and flowers in her hair.

The door had been left open, and presently she shouted, "Go upstairs! First on the left." The door of "first on the left" was ajar, and a baby was squalling inside. I knocked, and went into the most dishevelled room it is possible to imagine. There was a big bed in it, unmade, the bed-clothes tumbled anyhow, several broken chairs, and a washing-stand with a basin out of which some one had taken a bite. The novelist, in a dressing-gown open at the neck, and showing plainly that there was nothing but skin beneath it, was writing at a desk, throwing off his sheets as fast as he covered them. A very pretty little Irish girl, of about nineteen or twenty, picked them up as they fell, and sorted them, at the same time doing her best to quiet the baby who sprawled all over her, as she sat on the floor. They stood up when I came in, and the novelist tried to apologise for the disorder, but the baby howled so loudly that it was impossible to hear him.

"Take it out!" he shouted to the girl, and she obediently picked it up and carried it out of the room.

"That was a very good essay of yours, young man, and I thank you for it. I scarcely thought you would be as young as you are. How young are you?"

I told him.

"Fortunate fellow. Old enough for wine, and too young for liqueurs. The best of all ages. I hope you thank Jupiter every morning for your youth. Ah me, what it is to be young! I was a strapping fellow when I was as young as you. And now! Oh, you fortunate young dog!" He thumped his broad chest, that was covered with thick black hair, as I could see, for the dressing gown had fallen partly open. His big eyes twinkled under their strong dark brows, and he suddenly buried a huge unwashen hand in his curly black hair.

"Aha! You are thinking that it is not worth while to be a success, if this is all it leads to. Eh! What? Yes. I am right. I can always tell. That is the curse of it. Look at my wife, for example. She loves me. Yes. But she does not guess that I know she looks upon me as a big bull baby, very queer and mad, but so strong that it has to be humoured. In fact, when she carried off that vociferous little Victor Hugo, she was only looking upon you as a lamb offered providentially for sacrifice in place of Isaac. She is always afraid I shall throw Victor Hugo out of the window. It is very annoying to know that she feels like that. Funny woman. Pretty, don't you think? But what about that wine? If you go and shout 'Mrs. Gatch!' at the top of that staircase, the she-dragon who runs this place will come and bring up a bottle of something or other. I would shout myself, but you are younger than I."

I crossed the landing and shouted for Mrs. Gatch. Presently she stood below me in the narrow hall.

"Well, and what is it?" she asked crossly.

I was just going to reply, when the voice of the novelist bellowed from his room, like the voice of one of the winds of God.

"Mrs. Gatch, you are a bad-tempered woman. Don't deny it. Bring me a bottle of the best bad burgundy you have in the filthy cellar."

It was clear that Mrs. Gatch was frightened of him, for she brought the bottle at once, wiping it on her apron as she came into the room. We drank out of a couple of glasses my great man brought from a box in the corner. Then he talked of literature, and so well that the untidy bed, the unclean room, the wife and the baby were as if they never had been. In spite of his unwashen hands, in spite of the dressing-gown, he won his way back to greatness. He lifted the tumbler magnificently to watch the ruby of the wine, while he talked of Edgar Allan Poe, and of his methods, and of that wonderful article on the principles of composition. Poe was profound, he said, to have imagined that article, but the article represented him profounder than he really was. From Poe we came to detective and mystery tales, Gaboriau, Sherlock Holmes, and the analytical attitude, and so to the relations between criticism and art. It was a most opulent conversation.

I sat on a three-legged chair where I could see out of the window, and presently noticed the novelist's wife walking up and down on the opposite pavement, carrying the child and a blue parasol. She had not troubled to put on a hat, and she was evidently waiting till we had done our talk. It was clear that they had no other room. And so, regretfully, calculating a time that would leave her at the top of the street, while I escaped at the bottom, not wishing to put her to confusion, I told the novelist of an appointment with my editor, shook hands with him, was pressed to come again, ran downstairs, and walked away up the street. I walked quickly away, but not so quickly that I did not see the little woman hurry back into the house with Victor Hugo, to resume, doubtless, her occupation of sorting the pages of deathless prose that her "big bull baby" dropped from his desk.

* * * * *

I saw him more than once there later, and always the room was in the same condition, the child howling, the wife pretty, untidy as ever, the great man unwashed but working. How he could work! Sheet after sheet used to drop from his desk. Sometimes when I called upon him he would be in the middle of a chapter, and then he would ask me to sit down and smoke, while his pen whirled imperturbably to the end. He could write in any noise, and he could throw off his work completely as soon as the pen was out of his hand. He was quite contented in the lodging-house, living with wife and child in a single room. He seemed more amused than annoyed by its inconveniences. "After all," he would say, "I have to pretend to superb intellect, and the pretence would be exposed at once if I let such things worry me."

* * * * *

One day I had a post-card from him, saying he was going abroad. I did not hear from him again for several years, when a letter that came in a crested envelope told me he was settled in a flat. Would I come to dinner?

He was in Bloomsbury again, but the flat

was more comfortable than the room. It was very decently furnished, and quite clean. A book of his, that had had a great success in America, was the explanation of his magnificence. The door was opened by an elderly housekeeper, and I was ushered into his study with considerable ceremony.

He rose to greet me, but sat down again at once, and said that he was very ill.

I said I was sorry to hear it.

"Damn you, young man! You can afford to be. Look at you, you young bullock, and then look at me—a miserable wreck."

He lay back in his chair, with his black hair crisp and curly, his cheeks red and healthy, and his heavy black eyebrows stiff and strong over his active eyes. He was dressed, except that he had not a collar, and the muscles of his throat were as fine and beautiful as those of a statue. I could not think of him as ill.

But from time to time he reached languidly to the table, and took a tumbler of yellow opaque liquid, from which he drank a little, and then, after making a wry face, put the tumbler back.

Presently he explained. "Have you heard," said he, "that a great doctor, a man called Verkerrsen, has been investigating the long life of the Hungarians, and attributes it to the quantities of sour milk that they drink?"

I had not heard.

"Yes," he went on. "The whole matter is

explained in an article in the *Medical Journal*. You had better read it." He took a sip from the tumbler, and made a horrible grimace. "Ugh!" he said, "but I think the Hungarian sour milk must be nicer than the sour milk of London. Ugh! Disgusting. But I *must* take it, I suppose."

He loved theories above everything else, and went on sipping heroically till he finished the glass. Then he jumped to his feet, and arched his biceps, and smote proudly on his chest. "Ah!" he cried, "it was worth it. I feel better already. Let's have supper."

Supper was brought in, admirably cooked, and laid on the study table. We sat down to it with the elderly housekeeper. The novelist, restored by sour milk to ebullient health, was as happy as could be, joking now with her, now with me, talking most joyfully. Something crossed his mind, when he was half way through his soup, but it was no more than the shadow of a bird flying over a flower-bed in the sunlight. He bent towards me. "I say," he said, "my wife is dying in Dublin this week. Pass the toast."

I did not know what to reply. But there was no need, for he had passed on instantaneously to a new ingenious notion of his, that everything was a brain, that molecules were brains, that we were aggregations of tiny brains, that the world was a huge brain with us as parasites upon it, and that the universe, made up of brains, was nothing but a mighty brain itself.

He could think of nothing else till supper was done.

Then, when the housekeeper had cleared away the supper things, he went to the cupboard and pulled out two long narrow stands, each holding a dozen liqueur glasses. "My own idea," he explained, and proceeded to place upon the table one by one a dozen different bottles of liqueurs—Chartreuse, Benedictine, Crème de Menthe, Anisette, Cherry Brandy, and several with fantastic names of his own invention. "Let us drink each liqueur to a different genius," he said. "Chartreuse for Alexandre mon cher Dumas, Benedictine for the noble Balzac, Cherry Brandy for Fielding, Anisette for Sterne, Crème de Menthe—dull stuff, Crème de Menthe; we'll drink Crème de Menthe to—to—to Samuel Richardson. He'd have thought it so naughty."

There was a curious point about this man. He loved the bravery and show of conviviality, but he was not a Hans Breitmann to "solfe der infinide in von edernal shpree." He never got "dipsy," and he hated drunkenness above all other vices. The only time we quarrelled was when, hearing that I was going to see him, another man whom I scarcely knew forced himself upon me, and had to be introduced. The great man plied him with liqueurs till he fell on the floor, and quarrelled with me for six months because he had to help to carry the fellow to his lodgings.

I should like to see him again, but Bloomsbury has been the poorer for some time, being without him. I think he is in France. I never dared ask if the wife lived or died. It would have been so difficult to find the correct manner. Something like this, I suppose: "By the way, that wife of yours; underground or not? Pass the cigarettes."

A PAINTER

A PAINTER

THE painter had a studio made of two rooms, one, long and dark, opening into the other, which was larger, but kept in a perpetual twilight by shades over the window. The walls were covered with dark green curtains, and on them were hung weird, fiery-coloured pictures, compositions for Oriental dreams: two peris caressing a peacock by a golden fountain; a girl in crimson and gold holding fantastic wine-glasses towards the shadow of a man; a sketch in pastels of a pair of struggling gods. All round the floor, leaning up against the walls, were unfinished canvases, half realised dreams that had not the energy to get themselves expressed before they were forgotten, and other dreams, to be abandoned in their turn, were striving for the light. There was an old piano in a corner, and a sofa, a dark wood table, and some ebony chairs.

He was a small man, with hair not long, but very curly, beautiful eyes, and a little moustache. He dressed neatly, though he had less money for the purpose than most of the other artists in the building. He worked entirely alone, and laughed quietly at the anxiety of people who wished to succeed, to exhibit, to be publicly recognised as painters, unless he understood that they looked upon success only as guarantee of bread and butter. He could understand that people might, without degradation, work for bread and butter, and he always said he was willing to do so himself. But he never did. Chances came to him, as they come to everybody; but either the would-be purchaser was not appreciative, or he chose the wrong things to commend. The painter could never have slept with the thought that one of his pictures, an arrangement in colours, was in the house of a gold-watch-chained plutocrat who loved it for the sake of a story he had happened to read into it. He would have counted the picture as wasted, and would not have let it go to such a man, even if the money would have saved him from starvation.

There were only two very small exhibitions where he felt he could show his pictures with a free conscience, and he had a painting in each every year; and yet, though he had the year in which to paint them, his two pictures always went down unfinished. He used to paint on, dream after dream, imagining that each one was to be the annual masterpiece, and then, before any one of them was done, he would be started on another, until, a week before the exhibitions, he would find that he had not a single picture in such a state that he could expose it without shame to the eyes of other painters. Then he used to work furiously, first on one picture, then on another, now on the first again, until at the end of the week, almost in tears, he would send off the least unfinished of the lot, and, shutting himself up in his studio, refuse to allow any one to interrupt his self-accusation and remorse.

He called on me in my first lodging, and found me trying to play " Summer is icumen in " on an old wooden flageolet. But, although he was a musician, he asked me to come to his studio, to see his piano, which, very old, was a perfect instrument for the older music, Scarlatti, Corelli, and the Elizabethan songs. Very often after that he would play for hours in that dim room, while I listened, sitting and smoking over the fire. Sometimes another man used to come in and play the piano for him, so that he was free for the 'cello, that he handled with the love that is the greater part of skill. One winter we made friends with a model who had a violin. Then we used to keep Tuesday nights free for concerts: there would be the pianist, the artist round the corner in the large room playing the 'cello, and the pretty, fluttered little girl playing the violin in the long room by the fire, while I sat on the sofa and tried to keep time (for they could not see each other) by beating my foot on the floor. Sometimes all three would be together, and they were never more than two bars apart, and the caretaker who lived below the stairs used to thank us solemnly each night for the sweet music that we made. The painter made a sketch of her, the only humorous drawing he ever did, showing her seated in her chair, with her glasses in her lap, her hands clasped, her eyes turned up to the ceiling, entranced as if by a melody from heaven.

When we were tired of the music, the little model used to take the kettle from the cupboard, and make coffee for us, with a very pretty assumption of house-wifeliness and motherhood. Then, after the coffee, we would talk, and the painter used to sing old songs, or more often would sit content by the fire, watching the firelight bring out strange colours in the unrealised dreams that waited on the canvases against the wall.

His was a simple, earnest life, of a kind that is not so rare as books about studio life would make out. There are many like him, who care more for art than for recognition, and work on quietly, happily, living on bread and cheese, or going without it when painting materials become a more insistent necessity. Since those days he has become a success in spite of himself. Some illustrations he made to fairy tales interested people, and though he fled them when he could, and only asked to be let alone, he has become famous and almost opulent. But he lives as simply as before, and paints in the same manner. His pictures are all wonderful, but his patrons find it as difficult to get him to finish one as it is to persuade him to let it leave his studio when done. In the Middle Ages he would have been a monk and a painter of frescoes, loved by all the gentle-minded folk who came to worship in the church where his dreams were painted on the walls. Now, except among the few who know him well, the best word I hear said of him is that he is a good artist but a criminally unbusinesslike man.

A GIPSY POET

A GIPSY POET

No one knew whence he had come. Only, he had stood one day, a slight, black-haired, black-eyed boy, on the doorstep of a publisher's office, shy to enter or to retreat, with a little manuscript volume of poems in his hand. By some chance the publisher himself happened to come out on his way to lunch, and asked what the lad did, waiting there on his threshold. On hearing the boy's reply, and glancing for a moment through the volume that was timidly held out to him, he took him to his club, gave him a good lunch, and asked a number of questions. He confessed afterwards that he had learnt nothing except, what could be seen at once, that the boy was of an odd kind. Of what kind he decided as soon as he had read the poems.

In a month's time the little book was published, and the grace, the finish, the freshness of the songs in it ensured at least a critical success. There was something in this little book that had not been written before, something of the open road seen from other eyes than those of townsman or the ordinary country poet. The phrases were not those of the casual observer. The hedges were real hedges, with blackberries in them, or good twigs for burning, or straight branches for switches or walking-sticks. The dark nights were not made in theatres, but were bad for travellers, good for thieves. Men and women were men and women of the open air. There was something in every poem in the book that had the real blood and spirit of the country, something that made the book different from every other volume of the season. It was praised in half a dozen of the best papers, and the publisher, proud of his little romance, gave dinner parties, inviting distinguished guests to meet his poet.

Before the interest in him that the book had caused had died away, some one, more practical and more benevolent than most admirers of young poets, had got the boy permanent work as librarian of a small library in town. He settled in here among the books and students, and worked steadily from the autumn of one year to the June of the next. He had made other friends besides the distinguished people. There were several lodgings of poets as young and less fortunate than himself, where he used to come in the evenings and read his verses aloud, in an effective sing-song way, the manner, so he said, in which he composed them. He loved to listen to the old stories of Morte d'Arthur and the Mabinogion, that used often to be read aloud in the evenings at these lodgings, and there was an Indian book called "Old Deccan Days," for whose stories of rajah and ranee he would ask again and again. Often he would come back some days after one of these readings with poems in which he had retold the tales and given them a fresh significance. For us he was always eerie; there was a motive in his poetry that could never be ours, an indefinable spirit of wandering, and of nights spent in the open or in the shadows of the moonlit woods. It was as if a goblin were our friend. Nothing that he did or said could have surprised us much.

When that June came, it was after a cold May. Winter had lingered later than usual, and June came with a sudden warmth and a sense of spring as well as of summer. One evening one of his friends called at the library to take him up to Soho to drink red wine, which he loved, and to talk and dine in one of the little restaurants. The library clerks told him that the poet had not been in the place either that day or the day before. He had left no message, and was not in his rooms. His landlady only knew that he had gone out very early in the morning two days ago, and had not returned to sleep. He had not come back the next day, and after that his friends took in turn to call every evening. They found it necessary to persuade his landlady that she had no right to sell his few possessions. Ten days later, as we were sitting at dinner at our usual small restaurant in Soho, he came in.

His clothes were dirty and ragged, and his boots were almost worn out. He had no money, he said, but he was going to the library in the morning, where some was due to him. He was skilful in parrying our urgent questions, and we scarcely knew if he wished us not to know where he had been, or if he were ignorant himself. But there was a brighter light in his eyes than we had seen since first he came among us, and a clearer ring in his voice.

For the rest of that year he worked regularly in the library, and read and wrote or saw his friends in the evenings. Sometimes when we were with him in the streets a man or a woman would speak to him in an odd tongue. He always pretended not to understand them, but we noticed that afterwards he contrived to be rid of us for the rest of the evening. We knew that somehow his life was not ours, but we liked him very well.

In the following May he disappeared again, though for a few days only. In June he went, and in July, returning each time tired out, happy, and secret, an insoluble enigma. There began to be troubles for him with the library authorities.

One evening in early August he was in a room in Chelsea, drinking and singing old songs. His face was flushed, and he was over-excited. The songs seemed a relief to him, and he sang one after another. At the end of the evening, after some one had sung one of the usual English songs, he jumped up waving his glass, and sang uproariously in a language we none of us understood. His face was transfigured as he sang, and he swayed his whole body with the rhythm of his tune. When he had finished singing he tossed the wine down his throat, looked queerly at us, and then laughed to himself and sat suddenly down.

Afterwards two of his friends walked with him to the Embankment, as he lived at that time in lodgings on the south side of the river. Just as they turned up over Battersea Bridge, a man and a woman stepped across the road and waited in the lamplight. The man had a cap over his eyes, and a loose necktie. He was very straight, and walked more easily than a loafer. The woman had a scarlet shawl. As the three of them went by, the poet humming a tune for the others to hear, the woman touched his arm, and he looked round into her face.

"Good-night, you fellows," he said to the two who were with him, shook hands with them, which was not his usual custom, and left them, and went off with that strange couple. They stood looking after him in surprise, but he did not turn.

He disappeared from Bohemia as mysteriously as he came. That was four years ago, and not one of us has seen him since that night. Perhaps he will walk in again, with his boots worn out and happiness alight in his face. Perhaps he is dead. Perhaps he is wandering with his own people along the country roads.

CONCLUSION

CONCLUSION

Crabbe wrote to Edmund Burke in 1781: "I am one of those outcasts on the world, who are without a friend, without employment, and without bread. I had a partial father, who gave me a better education than his broken fortune would have allowed, and a better than was necessary, as he could give me that only. . . . . In April last, I came to London with three pounds, and flattered myself this would be sufficient to supply me with the common necessaries of life till my abilities should procure me more; of these I had the highest opinion, and a poetical vanity contributed to my delusion. I knew little of the world, and had read books only; I wrote, and fancied perfection in my compositions; when I wanted bread they promised me affluence, and soothed me with dreams of reputation, whilst my appearance subjected me to contempt. Time, reflection, and want have shown me my mistake."

In 1817 he wrote to a young lady: "You may like me very well — but, child of simplicity and virtue, how can you let yourself be so deceived? Am I not a great fat rector, living upon a mighty income, while my poor curate starves upon the scraps that fall from the luxurious table? Do I not visit that horrible London, and enter into its abominable dissipations? Am I not this day going to dine on venison and drink claret? Have I not been at election dinners, and joined the Babel-confusion of a town hall? Child of simplicity, am I fit to be a friend to you? . . . ."

Bohemia is only a stage in a man's life, except in the case of fools and a very few others. It is not a profession. A man does not set out saying, "I am going to be a Bohemian"; he trudges along, whispering to himself, "I am going to be a poet, or an artist, or some other kind of great man," and finds Bohemia, like a tavern by the wayside. He may stay there for years, and then suddenly take post-horses along the road; he may stay a little time, and then go back whence he came, to start again in another direction as a Civil Servant, or a respectable man of business; only a very few settle down in the tavern, for ever postponing their departure, until at last they die, old men, still laughing, talking, flourishing glasses, and drinking to their future prosperity.

I have tried to show what life is like in this tavern on the road to success—this tavern whose sign, gaily painted—a medley of paint-brushes, pens, inkpots, and palettes, with a tankard or two in the middle of them—hangs out so invitingly over the road that no young man can pass it without going in at the door. With memories of the older times, and pictures of the life of to-day, I have done my best to get the spirit of it on paper; and it is clear, now that I have finished, that there is something left unsaid. I have not brought Bohemia into perspective with the rest of a man's existence, nor told what happens when he comes to leave it.

For it is not an uninterrupted succession of artifices to get hold of daily bread, drinking bouts, wedding parties, and visits to the studios and lodgings of friends—small meaningless pains and pleasures. These things are not ends in themselves. There is something behind the very extravagance of the costumes that we wear. Our life, our clothes are different from conventional life and fashionable clothes, but they are not different from whim or caprice. People do not make fools of themselves for the fun of the thing, except in France. They never do it in Bohemia. The secret of the whole is a need for the emphasis and expression of individuality. When a youth, brought up in ordinary family life, feels somehow that he is not quite like the others, that he also is one of the prophets, the very sign of his vocation is an urgent need of marking his differences. He may have an overwhelming desire to shock his nearest and dearest relatives—even that is excusable—perhaps he will leave "Tom Jones" on his mother's drawing-room table. The regularity, the routine, the exactness of his home life will be about his neck like a mill-stone, as he struggles to fly with wings where others walk. He will feel, perhaps without admitting it to himself, the horror of being indistinguishable from among the rest of the human ants about him, and, by growing long hair, and refusing to wear a collar, does his best to strengthen, not others so much as himself, in believing that his is a peculiar species.

And so, when he goes along the road with his manuscripts or his sketch-books, lonely but very hopeful, and sees that gay sign hanging out, and, looking into the tavern, catches glimpses of a hundred others as extravagant as himself, he tells himself with utter joy that here are his own people, and, being like every one else a gregarious creature, throws himself through the door and into their arms. There are no Bohemians in the desert.

As soon as he is with his own people, dressing to please himself, and living a life as different as possible from the one that he has known, the whole energy of his need for self-expression pours itself without hindrance into his art. (Only the wasters lose sight of the end in the means, and live the life without thought of what they set out to gain.) The mad pleasures of the life, even the discomforts, the possible starvation, have their value in being such contrasts to the precision of the home he has left. Material difficulties, too, matter little to him, for his interests are on another plane. He can escape from the harassing knowledge that his purse contains only twopence-halfpenny in the glorious oblivion of painting a picture or fitting exact words to an emotion. He has always a temple in his mind which the winds of trouble do not enter, and where he may worship before a secret altar a flame that burns more steadily and brighter with every offering he lays before it. More practical things disturb him very little: do you remember Hazlitt's saying when he and John Lamb "got into a discussion as to whether Holbein's colouring was as good as that of Vandyke? Hazlitt denied it. Lamb asserted the contrary; till at length they both became so irritated, they upset the card-table and seized each other by the throat. In the struggle that ensued, Hazlitt got a black eye; but when the two combatants were parted, Hazlitt turned to Talfourd, who was offering his aid, and said: 'You need not trouble yourself, sir. *I do not mind a blow, sir; nothing affects me but an abstract idea.*'"*

That is a very perfect illustration of the Bohemian's attitude towards reverses of fortune that are not concerned with the progress of his art. A picture ill painted, a stodgy article (oh, the torments of forcing life into a leaden piece of prose!), these will upset him, make him miserable, dejected, at war with all the world. But penury; why, that is but a little price to pay for freedom;

* B. R. Haydon's "Correspondence."

and squalor may be easily tolerated for the sake of an escape from convention.

* * * * *

And now to speak of the farewell to Bohemia; for the young man grows older, and perhaps earns money, and takes upon himself responsibilities to another goddess than the white Venus of the arts. It is a long time since "The Lady Anne of Bretaigne, espying *Chartier* the King's Secretary and a famous poet, leaning upon his elbows at a table end fast asleepe, shee stooping downe, and openly kissing him, said, *We must honour with our kisse the mouth from whence so many sweete verses and golden poems have proceeded*";* but women have still a fondness for poets and painters, and, not too critical of the value of the verses and pictures, are even willing to marry their authors, moneyless, untidy wretches as they are. But no sooner have they married than they begin to tame them. Even the maddest cigarette-smoking art student, when she has married her painter, takes him away from Bohemia, which is, as perhaps she knows without thinking of it, not the place for bringing up a family. The woman is always for stability and order; a precarious, haphazard, irregular, unhealthy existence has none of the compensations for her that it holds out to her husband. Not that she does not think of him, too; but she prefers to see him healthy

* Peacham's "Compleat Gentleman."

than a genius. Anyhow, the door into the registrar's office is the door out of Bohemia. Things are never quite the same again. Witness Lamb, writing to Coleridge: "I shall half wish you unmarried (don't show this to Mrs. C.) for one evening only, to have the pleasure of smoking with you and drinking egg-hot in some little smoky room in a pot-house, for I know not yet how I shall like you in a decent room and looking quite happy."

And then, too, whether she means it or not, the wife alters the man's view of the goal at the end of the journey. She is always on the side of the recognised success. The artist, however unruly, finds himself once a week wearing a frock-coat at an "at home" given by his wife to "useful people." He soon discovers that he must exhibit in the usual places, if only to please his lady. He makes fewer experiments, but settles down to adapt his technique to subjects that are likely to tell. He works harder, or at least more consistently, and has less time for other people's studios. He learns that he is not a god after all, but only a working man. The rebellious dreams of his youth die in his breast, and he ends a Royal Academician.

The writer, when he marries, learns that he must no longer trust to earning a living by accident, while he does his favourite work. There are two ways open to him: he may do an immense amount of criticism and journalism, and keep his originality for what leisure he can find, or he may make his best work the easiest to sell. To keep up his prestige at home he must become a popular author.

The worst of it is that in becoming a success you lose the sympathy of the friends you have left in Bohemia, and find that for them you are even as one of the abhorred Philistines, tolerated for old sake's sake, but no longer one of the fighting band.

On the other hand, if the young man does not marry, he finds as he grows up that he is less and less of a Bohemian. His individuality no longer needs for its emphasis expression in externals. His taste in talk becomes less catholic—he is bored by the extravagant young fools who are ready to say anything about everything they know nothing about. He is annoyed at last, unless he is so philosophic as to be amused, by the little people with their great pretences, their dignities without pedestals; and he finds, as he becomes less able to give them the homage they require, that they become annoyed with him, and can do very well without him, having new sets of young admirers of their own.

A novel, a book of poems, or a picture wins him some real recognition—and with it, perhaps, a rise in income. His relations, who have for so long neglected him as a black and errant sheep, discover a pride in him, and want to introduce him to their friends. He is compelled, as it were by circumstances alone, to wear better clothes, and to take what he is told is his place in society. With better clothes comes a snobbish but pardonable dislike of being seen with the carelessly dressed. He moves to more convenient rooms, has a napkin on his breakfast table, and is waked in the morning by a maid with hot water, instead of by an alarm clock. Who knows?—he may even rent a cottage in the country. A thousand things combine to take him out of Bohemia.

And it is better so. There are few sadder sights than an old man without any manners aping the boyishness of his youth without the excuse of its ideals, going from tavern to tavern with the young, talking rubbish till two in the morning, painfully keeping pace with a frivolity in which he has no part. Caliban playing the Ariel—it is too pitiful to be amusing. There are men who live out all their lives in Bohemia (to paraphrase Santayana's definition of fanaticism), "redoubling their extravagances when they have forgotten their aim." I am reminded again of my friend's saying, that of all bondages vagabondage is the one from which it is most difficult to escape. If a man stays in it too long, if he allows its garlands to become fetters, its vagaries to lose their freshness and petrify into habits, he can never get away. When I think of the deathbed of one of these old men—of the moment when he knows of a sudden that his life is gone from him, and that after all he has done nothing—I quicken my resolve to escape when my time comes, and not to linger till it is too late.

But now, in youth, it is the best life there is, the most joyously, honestly youthful. It will be something to remember, when I am become a respectable British citizen, paying income tax and sitting on the Local Government Board, that once upon a time in my motley "I have flung roses, roses, riotously with the throng." It will make a staid middle age more pleasant in its ordered ease to think of other days, when a girl with blue sleeves rolled to her elbows cooked me a dinner from kindness of heart, because she knew that otherwise I should have gone without it; when no day was like the last, when a sovereign seemed a fortune, when all my friends were gods, and life itself a starry masquerade. My life will be the happier, turn out what it may, for these friendships, these pot-house nights, these evenings in the firelight of a studio, and these walks, two or three of us together talking from our hearts, along the Embankment in the Chelsea evening, with the lamps sparkling above us in the leaves of the trees, the river moving with the sweet noise of waters, the wings of youth on our feet, and all the world before us.

OXFORD PAPERBACKS

Rod and Line

Arthur Ransome

This collection of highly entertaining articles on the curious habits of both fish and fishermen was originally published in the *Manchester Guardian* a few years before Arthur Ransome wrote *Swallows and Amazons.* Packed with amusing anecdotes and useful tips, it will appeal to any reader who shares Ransome's own obsession, as well as many who do not.

A Literary Pilgrim in England

Edward Thomas

Edward Thomas here roams England in search of the homes of some of our most famous writers: Blake, Shelley, Tennyson, Coleridge, Hardy, Cobbett, Borrow, Swinburne, Wordsworth, and many others. He quotes extensively from their works, illustrating how the landscapes and cities of their youth and maturity developed their idiosyncracies and influenced their art.

The Autobiography of a Super-tramp

W. H. Davies

Preface by George Bernard Shaw

This is the classic account of the poet W. H. Davies's adventures as a young man travelling around America and England at the turn of the century. His spare, evocative prose gives raw power to his experiences among tricksters, down-and-outs, and itinerant labourers, and makes the characters he encounters–New Haven Baldy, the Indian Kid, and Boozy Bob–unforgettable.

Lavengro

George Borrow

Now acknowledged as a classic, *Lavengro* is a book in which autobiography is inextricably linked with fiction. Borrow was an inveterate traveller with a taste for the outlandish. The restless spirit of the young hero of *Lavengro* leads him to strange lands and adventures with gypsies, rogues and thieves.

'One of the most remarkable literary oddities of the nineteenth century: an autobiographical fantasy journey.'—*Observer*

OXFORD PAPERBACKS

London Particulars

Memoirs of an Edwardian Boyhood

C. H. Rolph

For a boy in Edwardian London the streets were a lively and entertaining playground. C. H. Rolph's extraordinarily vivid memory enables him to depict in minute detail the customs, characters, and events of the time.

'A vivid piece of social history'—*Observer*

'C. H. Rolph's writing is characteristically clear and sharp, springing into life and humour the people of the streets, and the children of his schools and their pastimes'—*Guardian*

The Rise and Fall of a Regency Dandy

The Life and Times of Scrope Berdmore Davies

T. A. J. Burnett

Foreword by Bevis Hillier

In 1976 a trunk more than 150 years old was discovered in a London bank vault. It had belonged to Scrope Berdmore Davies, one of the colourful characters in the legendary circle that surrounded the young Byron. The trunk contained everything that Scrope might have needed to write his memoirs: notebooks of Byron and Shelley, letters, bills, court orders, and much more. T. A. J. Burnett uses this material to reconstruct in vivid detail the life and times of a Regency dandy.

TWENTIETH-CENTURY CLASSICS

The Unbearable Bassington

Saki

Introduction by Joan Aiken

Illustrated by Osbert Lancaster

Set in Edwardian London, Saki's best known novel has as its hero the 'beautiful, wayward' Comus Bassington in whom the author invested his own ambiguous feelings for youth and his fierce indignation at the ravages of time.

'There is no greater compliment to be paid to the right kind of friend than to hand him Saki, without comment.'—Christopher Morley

A complete list of Oxford Paperbacks, including books in the World's Classics, Past Masters, and OPUS series, can be obtained from the General Publicity Department, Oxford University Press, Walton Street, Oxford OX2 6DP.